The
EMMETT TILL BOOK

Emmett "Bobo" Till and his mother

This little boy . . . just a little piece of

dust in the wind.

Mamie Till [Bradley] Mobley

M. Susan Orr Klopfer

Other books by M. Susan Orr Klopfer

Where Rebels Roost, Mississippi Civil Rights Revisited
(With Fred Klopfer and Barry Klopfer)
How Branson Got Started
301 Ways to Get Ahead (with Fred Klopfer)
At Ease With FoxPro
Abort! Retry! Fail! The DOS Answer Book
Internet Success with Fred (with Fred Klopfer)

See updates and book order information at

http://emmett-till.com

http://themiddleoftheinternet.com

In memory of

Joe Pullen, Emmett Till, Jo Etha Collier,

Cleve McDowell & Mr. and Mrs. Clinton Melton

PROLOGUE

Once exposed to the elements, the internal tissue of a lifeless body begins to decay, turning into gases and liquids. In water this process of decomposition occurs approximately four times faster.

So when they pulled the lifeless body of a young black teenager from the Tallahatchie River during the August heat back in 1955, only an initialed silver ring on his finger made identification possible.

Emmett Till had been stripped naked, pistol-whipped, shot through the head with a .45-caliber Colt automatic and barb-wired to a seventy-four-pound cotton gin fan before he was dumped into twenty feet of the muddy Tallahatchie River. Neither the killing nor the murder site generated much surprise. "That river's loaded with niggers," one old white man told reporters.[1]

FOURTEEN-YEAR-OLD TILL, once physically afflicted by polio, was kidnapped shortly after midnight on the twenty-fourth of August from his great-uncle's home in the small cotton town of Money, Mississippi.

He was driven away to a weathered plantation shed in neighboring Sunflower County, where at least two white men tortured and mutilated him. A witness heard his screams for hours until the two men finally ended Emmett Till's life.

What the young boy said to a white woman clerking at the small family grocery in Money will never be known. But Emmett Till's death became a civil rights milestone, setting off a chain reaction that would forever change the way we think and talk about race in this country.[2]

PART I The Crime

"The delta region had the highest number of lynchings in Mississippi during the period 1880 to 1930 and therefore, the highest in the nation. Ominously, Tallahatchie and Leflore County were at the top of the list…. It was into this volatile land, poisoned by decades of racism and paranoia, that a black Chicago teenager was placed for his summer vacation."

— *Mark Gado*

Delta cotton, ready for picking. In the 1950s, according to one former Delta sharecropper, it was not uncommon for crop dusters to spray directly onto the field laborers as they were chopping the weeds from the cotton fields. "They really didn't care. In fact they were trying to spray us," he said.

ONE LATE AUGUST NIGHT IN 1955 around a Boy Scout campfire burned down to its last embers, scoutmaster Robert Keglar and his campers heard a story they would not forget. A "very shaken" man came into camp in the early morning hours and told of hearing the screams of a teenage boy being tortured and beaten to death only hours earlier in a machine shed outside of Drew, over in Sunflower County.

There were horrible screams, the visitor said, and when the white men finished killing the young African American boy, they took his body from the barn and hauled it off. More than two men were in the lynching party, he told Keglar and others as the fire smoldered. Campers finally went to sleep and when they awoke for breakfast, the visitor was gone.

AT MIDNIGHT that same day, forty-six miles away from the scout camp, the parents of a seventeen-year-old Ruleville girl let early-morning visitors stay in their home for the night. J.W. Milam and Roy Bryant, the latter her mother's relative by marriage, were loud and nervous, she remembered.

"My parents didn't tell me then what was going on at the time. J.W. had a full brother, Bud, and I am very sure he was with them, too. I was in bed but I could hear their voices."

The woman, who asked to remain anonymous, said that years later her father told her that Milam and Bryant let him know what they had done to Emmett Till.

"They knew the law was looking for them. They also said that Carolyn Bryant was with them when they killed Emmett Till. I don't know when Bud joined them. I think they caught up with him later. He was a nicer person than his brother, and I don't think he would have killed someone – I hope not."

When she awoke at sunrise, all three men were gone. "I never knew what happened to them after they left our house. I think they knew the law was going to catch up with them. And I think they felt safe, since most of the officers were covering for them, anyway. I don't know if they turned themselves in, let themselves be found or if they were picked up by the sheriff and charged.

"I still can't believe how they put our family in such danger; there was so much turmoil after Emmett Till was killed. People in Drew – black and white – were threatening to kill each other's entire families. Some were threatening to kill as many as ten members of another person's family as payback."

"I know that my parents would have never covered for them. They came to our house and sat there all night. Later my parents told me what was going on. But I would never want anyone to think that our family helped them out."

"Most people in Drew and Ruleville felt the same way," she said. "After the trial, the only support for Milam and Bryant came from the Klan because they were members. Most people didn't want to have anything to do with them. They had killed a 14-year-old child, after all. Maybe they didn't mean to do it, but they did kill him."

*   *   *

So Many Affected …

U. S. Rep. John Lewis, D-Ga., said he was most affected by the death of 14-year-old Emmett Till, who was brutally tortured and shot in Mississippi in 1955. Lewis was 15 at the time.

"I remembered thinking that it could happen to anyone, me or my brothers or my cousins," said Lewis, a civil rights activist. "It created a sense of fear that it could happen to anyone who got out of line," he told Washington Post reporter Avis Thomas-Lester.[3]

Lynching touched all races and religions and occurred in all states in the mainland United States except for two in New England. Immigrants were frequent targets; at the beginning of the 20th century, the State Department paid nearly $500,000 to China, Italy and Mexico on behalf of lynching victims, Thomas-Lester reported.

"But the practice was predominant in the South, and four out of five victims were black, according to statistics compiled by Tuskegee University in Alabama."

* * *

Down in Greenville of Washington County, publisher Hodding Carter pulled a story off the newswire and placed it on the front page of his newspaper and then went about the rest of his work to get out his publication.

Two White Men Charged with Kidnapping Negro

Greenwood, Miss. (UP) – Two white men charged with kidnapping a 15-year-old [sic] Chicago Negro because they claimed he insulted the wife of one of the men, claimed today they released the missing boy unharmed. Sheriff George Smith said Roy Bryant, a storekeeper in nearby Money community and his half-brother, J.W. Nilan [Milam], were held on kidnap charges in the mysterious disappearance of Emmett Till of Chicago. They were arrested yesterday …

The world would awaken to the story of this young visitor who had left his Chicago home on August 20, 1955, to visit relatives in Money, Mississippi, a tiny cotton hamlet (population 100) on the eastern edge of the Delta. Emmett Till's trip was planned to be a summer vacation with relatives in the Delta countryside. It ended up in his murder.

Till's mother, Mamie Carthan [Till Bradley], was born to John and Alma Carthan in the small town of Webb, not far from Money. When she was two-years-old, her family moved to Illinois.

Emmett never knew his father, who was shipped out to Europe as an Army private. Mamie and Louis Till separated in 1942. But his father's silver ring was given to young Till as a remembrance.

Prior to his journey into the Delta, Emmett's mother cautioned him to "mind his manners" with white people. She told her boy not to fool with white people down there: "If you have to get on your knees and bow when a white person goes past, do it willingly."

Till's mother understood that in Mississippi race relations were a lot different than in Chicago. In Mississippi, over 500 blacks had been lynched since 1882, and racially motivated murders were still not unfamiliar, especially in the Delta where Till was going to visit. Racial tensions were also on the rise after the United States Supreme Court's 1954 decision in *Brown v. Board of Education* to end segregation in schools.

After *Brown*, there had been some hope, but "at the same time we thought we were making progress, the forces of reaction geared up to make progress of their own," NAACP leader Aaron Henry later wrote. Robert "Tut" Patterson, a World War II veteran like Henry and also of Clarksdale, reacted to *Brown* by forming the first Citizens' Councils, established to halt integration in Mississippi.

Patterson's goals were to make it impossible for any black or white person favoring integration to find or keep a job. Credit would be cut or mortgages would not be renewed of any person fighting against segregation. As the Citizens Councils grew in number, any interracial cooperation died and the terror increased. Groups such as the Regional Council of Negro Leadership, of which Henry helped to form, were forced underground. It was hoped by white council members that economic pressure would make blacks cooperate and that any whites fighting segregation would be halted by social and political pressure.[4]

Brown II, the Supreme Court's "implementation decision," came in May of 1955 and was followed by the NAACP's petitions for desegregation of the public schools in Vicksburg, Natchez, Jackson, Yazoo City, and Clarksdale.

Once the petitions were handed in, the names and addresses of all petition signers were published in local newspapers, with accompanying stories alerting communities these people were "agitators" and "trouble-makers." Some signers were forced to leave the state; others could not buy basic staples or work supplies. Aaron Henry provided a glimpse of what life was becoming like for those who tried to bring positive change to Mississippi:

> The Citizens' Council was sweeping the state and picking up momentum steadily. An air of fanaticism prevailed, and it almost seemed as if the whites had gone insane. Soon, even white people who had been willing initially to accept the decision hardened their positions. Some whites who joined the council did say that they did so to keep the radical element under control. The names of people who signed school petitions across the state were given to banks and other credit agencies with the suggestion that credit be denied to signers. Intimidation and job loss soon reached such proportions that many signers removed their names. The council was not subtle in its approach and announced frequently in newspapers that they would continue dealing with us through economic reprisals: "Not the lash, not the rope, we'll starve 'em out."[5]

By now, black voter registration numbers were falling as the intimidation increased. In Belzoni, Rev. George Lee and Gus Courts, NAACP and RCNL leaders in their community, refused to remove their names from the voting rolls at the demand of Citizens Councils members. Courts was evicted from his grocery store, pressured by the building owner, and then in May, Rev. Lee was shot to death in his car. A Coroner's jury ruled that Lee had died of causes unknown. Sheriff Ike Shelton investigated and said the pellets found in Lee's head were fillings in his teeth. Shelton's final report asserted that Lee was shot by another black after an argument over a woman.

In August, Lamar Smith was shot down and killed in the middle of the day in Pike County as he was working to register voters. Three white men were indicted for murdering Smith but they were never brought to trial. The circuit judge, Tom Brady, had authored the white supremacist tract *Black Monday.* According to Brady, it was impossible in Mississippi to get a white man to testify against another white man for a crime against a black. He was dead on.

WITH HIS MOTHER'S warning and wearing the ring that had belonged to his deceased father, on August 20, 1955, only three weeks after the murder of Lamar Smith, Till set off with his cousin Curtis Jones on the passenger train to Mississippi.

When Till and Jones arrived on August 21, they stayed at the home of Till's great-uncle, Moses Wright that was on the outskirts of Money, Mississippi.[6]

On the afternoon of August 24, the boys drove Wright's car into the small town of Money and stopped at the only grocery store to buy some candy.

Just before they entered the Bryant store according to his cousin, Till pulled out some pictures of his white friends in Chicago, and showed them to some of the local boys hanging around outside of the store, one story goes. The boys dared their Chicago visitor to talk to Carolyn Bryant, the store clerk. Till went inside and bought some candy, and what happened as he was leaving is unclear. The young man might have said, "Bye, baby" before he whistled at Carolyn Bryant.

Neither one of the young boys understood the enormity of what Till had done so they did not tell Moses Wright what had happened. Three days passed without incident. But on the fourth day, early Sunday morning, Roy Bryant, Carolyn's husband, and J.W. Milam, Roy's half-brother, knocked on the door of Wright's home.

With a pistol and flashlight in hand, they asked Mose Wright whether three boys from Chicago were staying with him. Wright led them to the room where Till was sleeping, and the men told Till to get dressed. Wright unsuccessfully pleaded with them to just whip Till.

As Milam and Bryant were leaving, they threatened Wright that if he told anyone they would kill him. But several hours later, Mamie Till was notified of her son's kidnapping. A search of the area was conducted, and Mamie Till notified Chicago newspapers of her son's disappearance. Wright told Money's sheriff the names of those who had taken Till, and the sheriff arrested Bryant and Milam on charges of kidnapping.[7]

There was no doubt that something had happened between Till and Carolyn Bryant when he and his cousin went inside the small Money grocery story owned by the Bryants. Carolyn Bryant later asserted that Till had grabbed her at the waist and asked her for a date. She said the young man also used "unprintable" words. He had a slight stutter and some have conjectured that Bryant might have misinterpreted what Till said. Others say that he could have been mildly retarded and any unexpected behavior on his part might easily have been misconstrued. Several black youths, all under 16, were reported to have been with Till in the store and according to one newspaper account, forced him to leave the store for being "rowdy."

By the time twenty-nine-year-old Roy Bryant returned to Money from a road trip three days after his wife's encounter with Till, it seemed that everyone in Tallahatchie County knew about the incident, every conceivable version, and Bryant decided that he and his half-brother, J. W. Milam, 40, would meet around 2:00 a.m. on Sunday to "teach the boy a lesson."

Around 2:30 a.m. Sunday morning, August 28, Bryant went to the Mose Wright home on the outskirts of Money and demanded to talk with Till. Both he and Milam forced their way into the back bedroom where Till was sleeping, woke him up and made him go outside to the car.

That was the last time anyone in his family saw Till alive. Within one day, perhaps setting a Mississippi record for a white on black crime, officers from Tallahatchie County and nearby Leflore County arrested Roy Bryant and J. W. Milam and charged them with kidnapping, while Sunflower County officials stayed away from the incident.

Both men first admitted they had taken the boy from his great-uncle's home but claimed they turned him loose the same night. Word got out that Till was missing and soon NAACP civil rights leaders Medgar Evers, the state field secretary; and Amzie Moore, head of the Bolivar County chapter, became involved, disguising themselves as cotton pickers and going into the cotton fields in search of any information that would help find the young Delta visitor.

* * *

"... Get the FBI on the case ..."

August 30, 1955

To: Mr. Gloster B. Current, Director, Branches NAACP, New York, New York

From: Medgar W. Evers, Field Secretary, Mississippi

On Sunday, August 28 at 2 A.M., a fourteen year old Negro boy, Emmett Till of Chicago, was forced from his home at Money, Leflore County {sic}, Mississippi, by three white men and a white woman who alleged that Till had made remarks that were displeasing to a white grocery owner's wife. One man has been apprehended by the Sheriff of Leflore County, the other man is being sought. If it is possible to get the FBI on the case, maybe we can get some results.

* * *

After collecting laborers' first hand, Amzie Moore, a civil rights veteran years since before World War II, surmised it was apparent that "more than 2,000 families" were murdered and lynched over the years, with their bodies thrown into the Delta's swamps and bayous.

Some believed that relatives of Till were hiding him out of fear for the youth's safety. Or that he had been sent back to Chicago where he would be safe. Regardless, witnesses told the Sheriff that Mrs. Bryant identified Till as "the one" after which the group drove away with Till.

Bryant and Milam claimed they later found out Till was not "the one" who allegedly insulted Mrs. Bryant, and swore to Sheriff George Smith they had released the young Chicago visitor. They would later recant and confess, after the trial ended.

HODDING CARTER, one of only a handful of Mississippi journalists striving for objectivity in race-related reporting, followed up the next day with a second UP wire story reporting that a 17-year-old fisherman, Robert Hodges, found Till's decomposed body barb wired to a seventy-four-pound cotton gin fan and floating in the Tallahatchie River some 12 miles north of the community of Money.

The bayou near the machine shed where 14-year-old
Emmett Till was killed.

PART II After the Murders

When they found his body, it was apparent that Emmett Till had been stripped naked, pistol-whipped and shot through the head with a .45-caliber Colt automatic before he was thrown into the muddy river. In an editorial on Friday, September 2, Greenville journalist Hodding Carter asserted that "people who are guilty of this savage crime should be prosecuted to the fullest extent of the law," a brave suggestion for any Mississippi newspaper editor to make and remain out of harm's way, Carter included.[8]

National media attention surrounding the young man's death, the trial and the inevitable acquittal of Till's killers, would have a broad effect on civil rights that no one could have imagined or predicted in becoming a key factor in the explosive year that launched the modern Civil Rights Movement..

Trees shelter the shore of a small Delta lake
near Greenville in Washington County.

EMMETT TILL'S BODY WAS first taken to Greenwood in Leflore County, even though his body was found in Tallahatchie County (after he was killed in Sunflower County). Then it was moved back to Tallahatchie County by an undertaker in Tutwiler to be embalmed and shipped by rail to Chicago. (The trial of Bryant and Milam took place in Tallahatchie County, where Till's body was found.)

Woodrow Jackson of Tutwiler cannot forget the day he was assigned to embalm Till. His boss got the call and instructed Jackson, a black, to drive 42 miles over to Greenwood to pick up the young man's corpse and bring it back to the Tutwiler Funeral Home.

"There was a patrol car in front and another one in back. Billy Ray Cole, a state highway patrolman from Tutwiler, told me not to stop for anything, and I didn't," Jackson said. He reached Tutwiler at approximately 4 p.m. and worked on Till's body all through the night, until 8 the next morning.[9]

"It was terrible and that's why it took a long time. I remember thinking his body must have been in the water for three or four days, and maybe longer. It was clear to me that he died from blows to the right side of his head."

When Jackson finished his work, "We put his body in a shipping case and sent him home to Chicago by train. I never met his mother, but I always hoped I helped her in some way."

IN CHICAGO, HORRID pictures of the young man's corpse soon appeared in *Jet* magazine, drawing national and international attention. Over 100,000 people walked by Till's open casket before the funeral took place; hundreds of thousands read about his murder. Emmett Till's mother insisted the world see what was done to her son.

While Mamie Till experienced difficulty in getting her son's body shipped out of the Delta, she had already made the decision to have an open casket funeral. Mamie wanted the world to know that her son's right eye was missing, his nose was broken, and there was a hole on the side of his head. *Jet* magazine ran photos of Till's body. Fifty thousand people attended the funeral and soon the Mississippi Delta murder became an international story.

But down home in Sunflower County, Milam and Bryant were gathering support. Whites in their community claimed the two men were innocent, and contributed to their defense fund, filling up the money jars that had gone up in the small grocery stores and gas stations.[10]

RUMORS KEPT CIRCULATING about Emmett Till's death, especially in Drew, only a few miles away from the small machine shed where Till was taken, tortured and murdered. From the start, the whisperers held that a woman's voice was heard in the dark when Till was taken from his uncle's home.

"There were so many rumors. We all knew right away that Emmett Till was killed in Sunflower County and not over in Tallahatchie County," the retired Tutwiler embalmer said. "There were others involved besides Milam and Bryant. And we knew that some of the witnesses were held in Charleston's jail during the trial."

Mose Wright, before he died, had also claimed hearing a woman's voice from the truck; Wright was Till's great-uncle and was at home when Milam and Bryant entered the house to get Till. Simeon Wright, his son, who later became a Chicago minister, told of hearing his father talk about the crime and involvement of a woman, saying:

"They took Emmett out to the truck to ask, 'Is this one?' And a female voice said "Yes."

A conversation among friends ...

Like countless black males before him, Emmett Till received the ultimate punishment for threatening Mississippi's rigid Jim Crow laws of racial behavior. In the past, the press would have ignored such a killing. However, this time it was very different for several reasons, several black Delta residents said.

"He was just a kid, that's why this murder was so different than all of the rest." Nettie Davis of Drew makes her point for a second time during an early evening conversation. Davis and others are patient in offering their northern guests what facts they know about Emmett Till's murder on this cool, fall evening forty-eight years after the murder.

Their memories bring a fresh reality to the story this night. You need to understand. There had been other murders. Joe Pullen, George Lee. Horrible murders. But Emmett was a young boy, just 14, and he didn't know the rules. "Emmett's mother said she tried to tell him, but he couldn't have really understood how much different things were in the Delta than they were in Chicago," Davis states.[11]

How could black parents ever protect their children in those days? What if you had a precocious child who might be misunderstood? How would you keep a child quiet? And safe?

"Well, you didn't take your children out very much," one man offers. "You tried to protect them by keeping them away from places where they could get into trouble or be hurt or see something bad. But you didn't want to talk a lot about these things, because a child shouldn't have to be so scared."

A friend of Davis's remained on the periphery of this conversation, but then pulled in his chair closer and began to talk of his own experiences regarding his sister and the crime against Emmett Till.

She was also fourteen years old at the time of Till's death and was a student at the Drew School. She was so traumatized and angry at the time, she has never spoken to a white person since, he said. Maybe it would be good for his sister, if she would speak to someone now about her feelings.

He drew out his cell phone and offered to try and set up an interview with her. After a few rounds over the phone with her brother, the sister said she *might* talk after all. An appointment was made for a week later but fell through when she backed out on the morning of the scheduled interview.

THE MAN'S SISTER WAS not alone in her trauma. Mississippi writer Ann Moody in her autobiography recalled her own reactions and those of other youngsters around her when hearing about Till's murder. Moody was walking to her after-school job the evening she heard the news:

> There was a whole group of us, girls and boys, walking down the road headed home... However, the six boys in front of us weren't talking very loud ... they were just walking and talking among themselves.

> All of a sudden they began to shout at each other.... "That boy wasn't but fourteen years old and they killed him. Now what kin a fourteen-year-old boy do with a white woman?"

"That boy was from Chicago…. He probably didn't even think of the bitch as white."

I walked up to one of the boys. "Eddie, what boy was killed?" "Moody, where've you been?" he asked me. "Everybody's talking about that fourteen-year-old boy who was killed … by some white men…"[12]

Employed as a domestic servant by "one of the meanest white women in town," Moody was confronted the moment she reached her employer's home:

Mrs. Burke entered the kitchen.
"Essie, did you hear about that fourteen-year-old boy who was killed…?" she asked me.
"No, I didn't hear that," I answered, almost choking on the food.

"Do you know why he was killed? He was killed because he got out of his place with a white woman. A boy from Mississippi would have known better than that. This boy was from Chicago. Negroes up North have no respect for people. They think they can get away with anything. He just came to Mississippi and put a whole lot of notions in the boys' heads here and stirred up a lot of trouble," she said passionately.

"How old are you, Essie?" she asked me after a pause.
"Fourteen. I will soon be fifteen, though," I said.
"See, that boy was just fourteen too. It's a shame he had to die so soon."[13]

Moody went home "shaking like a leaf on a tree." Mrs. Burke had tried to instill fear within her many times and had given up. "But when she talked about Emmett Till there was something in her voice that sent chills and fear all over me. Before Emmett Till's murder, I had known the fear of hunger, hell, and the Devil. But now there was a new fear known to me – the fear of being killed just because I was black. This was the worst of my fears."

* * *

Aaron Henry would recall in later years hearing about Till's murder; the news came just three weeks after Lamar Smith was killed in McComb over voter registration.

Rumors were circulating that someone in Drew [Sunflower County] had seen Till in the back of a pickup truck early one morning and that the two men were seen stealing the gin fan that was ultimately found tied around Till's neck.

Aaron Henry immediately drove over to Mound Bayou to tell Dr. Howard, who went to Sheriff Sandy Smith of Leflore County, where Milam and Bryant were being held on the kidnapping charges.[14]

In his biography, Henry recalled that he and others were asking that the trial be postponed for several days in light of new and still-developing evidence. "Sheriff Smith and Attorney Stanley Sanders refused and said that the trial would proceed as scheduled."[15]

During a press conference in Mound Bayou called by Dr. Howard, reporters were told that more evidence was uncovered in the Till case – that several people in Drew were potential witnesses. Howard also asked for a one-day postponement of the trial:

"Smith and Sanders realized the reporters would make a big story out of it, so they agreed to put off the trial for one day." That night, according to Henry, several people, including himself, went to Sanders' office in Drew and told him they were going to comb the area. "He told us that we were on our own if we were going to go looking for witnesses and that if we got shot, it was our business."[16]

Aaron Henry and others had heard about a cotton worker, Mamie Smith, who might know something about the murder,

> " … so Ruby Hurley, NAACP regional director from Atlanta, put on an old dress the next morning and went into the fields to pick cotton. We hoped she could get the story without being noticed. Mamie had seen two Negro boys on the back of a truck driven by Milam and Bryant, and the boys were holding something under a canvas. The boys' names were Collins and Loggins."[17]

Henry, Hurley and Amzie Moore talked to others living in the region who said they saw Milam and Bryant moving Till. The two were able to convince these witnesses to appear at the trial. "They told what they had seen, but the trial was not taken seriously … and the two men were freed," Henry said.

After the trial and exoneration of Milam and Bryant, both Henry and Hurley got word that Collins wanted to talk. "Considerable preparation was made for the meeting, and Alex Wilson [editor] of the Chicago Defender came down to get Collins out of the state if he wanted to go. We went to a restaurant in Tutwiler to meet the boy. He was frightened to death and said that he didn't know a thing….

"We insisted that he had been a participant and that perhaps he felt his life was in danger," Henry recalled. But Collins stayed with his story that he knew nothing. Wilson promised to take him from Mississippi if he would talk, and Collins agreed to "let us know something later on."

That night, Collins appeared at Henry's house, stating he wanted to go to Chicago. Wilson put Collins in his car that night, and

Collins' story later appeared in full in the *Defender*, but Milam and Bryant were already free, according to Aaron Henry.

Hank Klibanoof told this version:

> The verdict was not unexpected but upset Wilson nonetheless. He decided to stay on the case, to drive deeper into the Delta seeking the other witnesses. "The smooth hum of the auto motor did not dispel the danger involved in the mission," he later wrote in the Defender papers.
>
> "I was not shaken by fear. I had decided before leaving home, and after communing with God, that if I could in any way help to contribute anything to justice in this shameful case ... whatever the price, so be it."
>
> After four days that he described as harrowing, danger filled, Wilson finally tracked down one of the supposed witnesses, Levy Too Tight Collins, and drove him to Chicago to be questioned for two days by the newspaper's general counsel. For days, the Chicago and Memphis papers made an enormous splash with Wilson's coup and featured front-page photo- graphs showing Too Tight sitting with Sengstacke [John H. Sengstacke, the *Chicago Defender* publisher].
>
> In the end, Collins denied knowing anything about the murder. Wilson's articles made it clear he didn't believe Collins: "Collins' denial does not completely clear him of implication in our knowledge of the crime," Wilson reported.
>
> "There remains a haunting suspicion that Collins knows more than the Defender was able to elicit from him."

PART III The Trial

"If we in America have reached the point in our desperate culture when we must murder children, no matter for what reason or what color, we don't deserve to survive, and probably won't."

– William Faulkner

A Ruleville Church in Sanctified Quarters, where slaves once
lived. Ruleville, located between Drew and Money
in Sunflower County, was the home of civil rights leader,
Fannie Lou Hamer, who often talked of Till's murder.

Till's mother had received a letter three years before her son's murder from the United States Department of Defense informing her, without a full explanation, that her husband had been killed in Italy due to "willful misconduct."

Then two weeks before the Tallahatchie County grand jury met, noted racist and Sunflower County planter Senator James O. Eastland dug up this "information" on Louis Till's past and leaked it to the press. The U. S. Army, according to Eastland, had executed Private Till in Italy in 1945 for "raping two Italian women and killing a third." The insinuation was that Emmett's father's behavior ran in the family.

Mamie Till turned to the federal government for help but got none. She had not received her ex-husband's Army records, and now she wanted to know how a senator, but not a widow, could receive that information. She was refused a meeting with President Dwight Eisenhower and FBI Director J. Edgar Hoover wrote in a memo: "There has been no allegation made that the victim [Emmett Till] has been subjected to the deprivation of any right or privilege which is secured and protected by the Constitution and the laws of the United States..."

* * *

ASK FOR A TRANSCRIPT of the "Milam-Bryant" (or the "Emmett Till") trial at the Tallahatchie County Courthouse in Sumner and the clerk will say it does not exist: "We only keep transcripts when there is an appeal, and there never was one," she responds.

Tallahatchie County courthouse officials get at least a half-dozen such requests each year for the transcript but no longer have a case file on the Till trial. If there are any copies of the transcript – and no one knows for sure – "there are many different versions of who has a copy," according to Davis W. Houck, an associate professor in the Department of Communication at Florida State University, who involved his graduate class in tracking down the documents.

Delta lore is that an Itta Bena man, a friend of Till's mother, had the transcript, "but it was stolen by a prostitute" during an argument. "Everybody's got their own story, and the stories keep spinning out," Houck told an Associated Press reporter.

Charleston native Steve Whitaker wrote his 1963 political science master's thesis at Florida State on the Till case and at one time had a copy of the 320-page manuscript, given to him by lead defense attorney J. J. Breland. Whitaker believes there were "possibly up to three copies made."

As a researcher with the Florida Department of Health, Whitaker claimed his copy was ruined when his basement flooded in the 1970s "along with 1,000 letters, which then Tallahatchie County Sheriff Clarence Strider received during the trial."

His stepfather, N.Z. Troutt, was Charleston's chief of police at the time and provided security at the trial. Whitaker, a fifteen-year-old during the trial, attended one day: "There were a lot of people in the county who would have unquestionably voted guilty. But the particular people they picked for the jury, they were not going to convict, no matter what," Whitaker opined

TALLAHATCHIE COUNTY IS one of ten counties in Mississippi with two county seats – Charleston (named after the city in South Carolina) and Sumner, named after its pioneer settler. In 1902, the county was divided, and the second courthouse was built at Sumner, housing the records of lands in Tallahatchie County west of a line almost parallel with the Tallahatchie River.

Sumner, a quiet little Southern town separated by its near-pristine bayou, is part of the Second Judicial District and is set atop some of the most fertile land in the Delta. The Sumner courthouse was site of the Milam-Beckwith trial, while the county Sheriff reportedly kept witnesses locked up and isolated in the other county seat of Charleston. Some others say the "witnesses" were kept locked up in the Sumner jail.

Cassidy Bayou, one of the Delta's most scenic waterways, runs through Sumner flowing southward and is the longest stream in Mississippi because it is so crooked. On one side of the bayou stands Sumner's Baptist Church. Erected in 1917, its pews taken from the old Baptist church and slid across the bayou on the ice.

Across the bayou appears the small town's Presbyterian Church, designed after a great church in Paris and built in 1920.

The standing courthouse located in the center of the small business district was built in 1909. As with most Mississippi county courthouses, a somber monument to the memory of Southern confederate soldiers was erected four years later on the northeast corner of the courthouse square.

Here in historic Sumner – a mile and a half from the birthplace of Till's mother in Webb – was where the Milam-Bryant trial unfolded in the fall of 1955. Few visiting journalists would lose the irony of being greeted by the town's slogan emblazoned on a prominent sign: "Sumner – a good place to raise a boy."[18]

Scores of national reporters and photographers – white and black - would also remember Sheriff Strider, " … a big, fat, plain-talking, obscene-talking sheriff you would expect to find in the South," wrote John Herbers, representing the United Press.

Not used to caring after an international pool of journalists and photographers, the sheriff made sure black reporters were "provided" a card table off to the side. When Detroit Congressman Charles Diggs came to Sumner to observe the proceedings, Strider wouldn't allow him into the courtroom until the presiding judge made him do so. Then he escorted U. S. Rep. Diggs to the "Jim Crow" table where black reporters sat.

Opening Monday, September 19, and ending that Friday, this "first great media event of the Civil Rights Movement," as baptized by David Halberstam (then a young correspondent covering Mississippi) was attended by more than seventy reporters and thirty photographers.

IN THE FALL OF 2004, a gray-haired, white Sumnerite in her late eighties, Ada Guest, remembered attending the "Till" trial – "the biggest week in Sumner" – for one day as guest of her boss, a Sumner attorney who arranged for her to stand at the back of the courtroom.

"He told me this was something I should not miss. I remember the courtroom was crowded and it was so hot.

"Mostly I remember that Emmett Till's mother came to the trial every day; her car door was opened courteously by the black courthouse janitor each morning when she arrived at the courthouse."[19]

Mrs. Guest remembered seeing the black reporters working at a table separated from white reporters.

"The black Congressman [Diggs] was sitting by the black reporters," she said. Wives of the defendants sat with their husbands and their children stayed close by. "They played sometimes, and they slept and got cranky, too."

Dr. Howard of Mound Bayou whose life had been repeatedly threatened, had already hired armed bodyguards to protect himself and his family. During the trial, the physician extended this protection to the black witnesses and to Till's mother. After each black witness testified, Howard, Medgar Evers and other NAACP officials helped them slip out of town.

The all-white grand jury surprised most people in the first place by quickly ordering Bryant and Milam to stand trial. It was unusual in Mississippi for any action to be taken against whites who committed violence against blacks; it was not the first time a Mississippi court would hear a case of white men accused of murdering a black, but it would become the most famous.

A GROUP OF BLACK journalists quietly tried to help the prosecution team of District Attorney Gerald Chatham and Robert Smith, a former FBI agent appointed to assist by Gov. Hugh White because "the people of Mississippi are anxious that justice be done."

Hank Klibanoff, writing about L. Alex Wilson, a well-known black journalist who covered the Till trial, stated: "Even the harshest critics of Jim Crow justice believed that the prosecutor was making an earnest effort to convict the defendants and that the judge was being fair-minded in his handling of the case.

"But the sheriff's investigation was lackadaisical, and the prosecutor lacked witnesses that everyone in the black community knew existed: the field hands who had seen Till with the defendants in their truck, who had seen the truck drive into a barn, who had heard the beating and screaming, and who had seen the truck leave the barn and head for the river."[20]

Word was out that two of the field hands had been on the truck with Till, had been inside the barn during the beating and had been ordered to clean the blood from the barn floor.

Encouraged by prominent black leaders in the Delta, Wilson with several other black journalists decided to seek out the witnesses themselves; two white reporters were "brought into the hunt" as well – since their credibility with white law enforcement authorities would be needed in order to hand over the witnesses.

The reporters worked late into the night, as the trial was in progress, driving across the dirt roads through the flat cotton fields leading to the doors of sharecropper homes. "Eventually, the reporters pulled in three witnesses who reluctantly agreed to testify and who lent great weight to the prosecution's case. But the two who were said to have been inside the barn eluded the searchers."[21]

MANY REPORTERS OBSERVED the most dramatic moment in the Sumner trial came when Mose Wright, at the potential risk of losing his own life, named the two white men who kidnapped his great-nephew. Moses Wright was scared, and some thought he might skip town instead of testifying.

Only considerable effort on the part of Medgar Evers, the local NAACP agent at the time, had kept Wright from fleeing. "Wright received a number of threats saying that he would be killed if he took the witness stand. But without his testimony there was no prosecution case. Showing exceptional courage, he took the stand and named both Milam and Bryant," David Halberstam reported.

Defense attorney John C. Whitten tried pressuring the jurors in his closing statement, telling them "Your fathers will turn over in their graves if [Milam and Bryant are found guilty] and I'm sure that every last Anglo-Saxon one of you has the courage to free these men in the face of that [outside] pressure."

The jurors – all white – listened and then deliberating for all of 67 minutes returned a "not guilty" verdict on September 23rd, the 166th anniversary of the signing of the Bill of Rights. The jury foreman later explained, "I feel the state failed to prove the identity of the body." Identification of Till's body would remain an issue for some critics until 2005 when an autopsy was finally completed in Chicago.[22]

Some reporters reported overhearing laughter from inside the jury room and one juror later admitted, "We wouldn't have taken so long if we hadn't stopped to drink pop."

When the verdict was read, Milam and Bryant lit up cigars and kissed their wives in celebration. Some in the press corps wept when the jury acquitted Till's murderers. Pulitzer prize-winning journalist Hodding Carter described "the tension from the murder and trial" as "the worst" [he] had ever seen.

The Greenville publisher believed that matters were going to get "more violent down this way before things take a turn for the better," (a prediction made again sixteen years later by Delta leader Aaron Henry regarding lack of prosecution of a young black school girl killed in Drew, Jo Etha Collier). Carter told others he had never before felt quite as discouraged about racial relations and attitudes.[23] All along, Carter had called for punishment for the Till murderers, angering many Greenville residents who were firm in their racist positions.

After the trial and then following a grand jury's refusal in Leflore County to indict Bryant and Milam for kidnapping, to which they had confessed, Hodding would write one of his strongest editorials: The grand jury had ... "told the world that white men in Mississippi may remove Negroes from their homes against their will to punish them or worse, without fear of punishment for themselves" [and that Bryant and Milam] "admitted taking the boy from his uncle's home to punish him for insulting the wife of one of them meant nothing to the grand jury."

> Unfortunately, it is going to mean a great deal to Mississippi and none of it will be good. If this miscarriage of justice were an isolated incident we could be less ashamed of the present and less fearful for the future. But it is not unique. The records of our courts reveal a shocking number of related incidents. In one Mississippi county a Negro who raped a white woman has this year been executed, a fate he deserved, but the same day a white man was given a minimum jail sentence of two years for the heinous rape of a Negro child.[24]

Carter editorially stated that in another Mississippi county, "a grand jury was unable to indict the white slayers of a Negro political worker who was shot to death on the courthouse lawn, with a large number of people nearby, because no witnesses would testify."

Most of what was happening in Mississippi, Carter asserted, had "nothing to do with segregation," even though violence had "multiplied in the wake of the … Supreme Court … decision on segregation in the schools." This instead, was "naked racially-inspired terror" [that we] "are paying and will continue to pay a price for … both in the sight of God and our fellow man."[25]

* * *

Minister responds to the violence of the times

Following the murder of Emmett Till and acquittal of Bryant and Milam, a black McComb minister wrote to Lieutenant Governor Carroll Gartin in August of 1957 to suggest that something must be done regarding the violence against negroes. Rev. Hollis N. Turner's eight page letter (treated in an aloof manner by Gartin who sent "the negro's letter" over to Ney Gore of the Sovereignty Commission)[26] tragically goes through several rapes and murders perpetrated against people in or near Magnolia and McComb:

"Many more cases of such crimes and atrocities have been committed on the Negro race such as the Till murder and other cases in Mississippi and other southern states with no law protection for the colored race."

Turner tells of the unresolved case of Betty Butler who was "killed a few steps north of the overhead bridge" in McComb, "by a sixteen-year-old white boy. Or the Kidnap/murder of a 16-year-old white girl residing in Walthall County by four white men. The girl was taken from her bedroom, "carried into a river swamp and raped." One man confessed, but was acquitted by an all-white jury in a trial in Magnolia, he stated. No date was given but near the same spot, a twelve-year-old girl was "molested on Saturday June 29 of this year."

The younger girl was "near a place called Mesa helping a married sister of hers. She was scrubbing her sister's house when two white men drove up and stopped. They were drinking. Two of the children went out near the car and the girl called them back. The white men asked if those were her children. The girl answered 'no!'. After offering her a drink of beer, the men told the girl if those were not her children she would soon have one. The girl began crying. The men told her that there was no need of crying, and told her that she was going to get in that car. The girl ran out then to the milk dairy to her sister and brother-in-law and told them of this matter and they called the law."

No help from the law was received in these and other crimes mentioned, Rev. Turner asserted. "Another thing that keeps stirring up race trouble is the denial of full rights of citizenship to Negroes. It is neither fair nor right for us as a race of people to have to fight to defend a democracy that denies us the basic and fundamental rights guaranteed us by that democracy. Why should we have to fight on the battle fronts for liberty we never can have?" ... Instead of trying to outlaw the NAACP, why not put forth efforts to outlaw the evils that keep the NAACP at work trying to better conditions for the Negro race?"

Rev. Turner suggested representatives of the two races get together to work out their differences, noting "We can do this better for ourselves than outsiders can do for us."

IN 1959, SOVEREIGNTY Commission Records show that in a search to identify NAACP members in Pike County,

Turner is described by the investigator as "humble"
"helpful" "an opportunist" and "not overly endowed with
intelligence. In 1960, investigator Andy Hopkins is
advised to approach Hollist Turner as a potential informant
in Pike County.[27]

* * *

As a publisher with a strong sense of economic development,
Hodding Carter could see the population continued to dwindle in
Mississippi while in "our sister state it rises." It bothered him that
income lagged behind that of other Southern states and far behind
the rest of the nation, "and that 65 out of every 100 college graduates
in Mississippi leave the state for far more reasons than just greener
pastures."

What had occurred in Leflore County (referring to the grand
jury's later refusal to indict the two men on kidnapping) after the
Milam-Bryant acquittals in Tallahatchie County would surely come
back to haunt Mississippi. Carter believed. "It will be a long time
before Mississippi recovers from the injury the Leflore County grand
jury has done to our state and to humanity."

In her biography of the famous Mississippi Delta journalist,
Ann Waldron, a newspaper editor herself, observed that Carter could
write "a brave editorial like this and almost simultaneously blame the
North for the South's problems, as he did in an article for *The
Saturday Evening Post*." In Memphis six black men had beaten a white
man, kidnapped his companion, and raped her repeatedly. "Why
didn't the northern press play this up like the Till case? Carter asked.
"Why did the North blame a whole state for the Till murder?" There
was no doubt that Mississippians were convinced that they lived in a
'misunderstood and abused' state, Waldron observed.

Carter built a list of "newsworthy" events that had been
reported in the Delta Times (DD-T) but had not received publicity
up North:

"A young white woman had risked her life to rescue a black child from the same river in which Emmett Till's body was found. Greenville residents – whites and blacks together – had raised – more than $2,000 to send the black high school band, the only band invited from the state of Mississippi to participate in a Negro Elks convention parade in New York." The list went on.

"Hodding saw it as a hopeful sign that business-minded individuals were beginning to realize that the sizzling racial climate would not help Mississippi promote new industry…[but he would go on to conclude that] 'ours is a besieged state, but one not inclined to surrender. No one should expect that a decision of a Supreme Court can soon or conclusively change a whole people's thinking. That must be understood.'"

Still, local and statewide pressure on Hodding Carter grew "and Hodding showed it. He wrote to a friend who was going abroad as a Fulbright lecturer that he envied him. 'Right now I'd rather be at the North Pole than in Mississippi.'"

Explaining Mississippi culture to another friend, Carter told the conservative writer that "Southerners will generally treat you politely until they make up their minds to kill you."[28]

*　*　*

A very different version of the Emmett Till story arrives via e-mail in three separate messages.

11/5/2004 1:20:18 AM

Thank for writting this great Peice of history. I'm so glad to see your writing on these murders I cannot wait to see your book by it and put it in my fathers hand. I'm from Drew Mississippi my name is Shirley. I want to tell my fathers story of emit till.

He had a freind thats dead now that told the story his story was different he said that one of the Milan ladies had been riding emmit around spending time with emitt because he was retarded and she liked the boy and the man was mad at his wife and they told three men to get emmit and teach him a lesson and instead of these men teaching him a lesson they took him to a barn outside of Drew and beat him.

The place you can find it if you go through Drew by AW James school and follow the road pass the bridge on out pass ,the golf course .Drew Country club Keep that road straight on around you will see a big beatiful house surronded by 2 ponds and woods. It use to be an even bigger house back there with a barn and that is supose to be the place where Emmit Till was killed.

Do not go to far around when you pass that white church and the old tore up miller store you have passed it. The house is a beautiful house setting of to itself its a curve of the road.

The men were supposidly did this for just a jug of whiskey. The lady after seeing emitt all mutlated suposedly shot emitt and put him out of his misery that is when emitt was taken to moneys and dumped. There was a store in Ruleville a long time ago that belong to the milams it sat to the side of where Jug Burgers ,One stop is now this man told my fat have died here that the store went down because of the killing of Emitt no one would go to it. 3 of the men suposidly have beat emit t died .This is the story I was told as a child

I do not no what happen to emmit I'll just be glad when the truth comes out my dad is old and always beleived Emmit

was killed in Drew and he mentioned the death of Joe
Pullen and Joe eartha Love her father Paul love lives in
Ruleville and my father Knows him.

Cleve Mcdowell was my fathers lawyer and it hurt dad
when he heard how he died your book will make him feel
better. Your book is gonna be the best gift to him a peice of
history and I cannot wait to buy it and put it in his hands.

11/8/2004 12:31:11 AM

Hi, Sorry for being so late getting back to you. I had to talk
to my family about meeting you. I just left them and They
do not think its a good Idea so I have to say no. I'm sorry.
They believe that if it was a way to prove some of this or
any of this that it would be alright to talk to you. This was
just a story someone told my family years ago.

11/8/2004 2:27:14 PM

Your welcome but I promised my family I would leave this
alone so I can't meet you or dig in this anymore This will
be my last letter to you and thanks again for not using my
name. My family [removed] they were conserned about
there name being mention on something that may or may
not be true. They are all up in age and still believe in
people getting hurt about such information like this.

Just do me a favore don't stop writing about these deaths
your on a good start and there's a lot more to be
discovered. Drew has it's share of history and its ghost.
Don't thank me. Thank you for this opportunity.
[name removed by request]

• * *

39

PART IV REACTIONS

RESPONSE AROUND THE Delta and Mississippi to the entire Emmett Till murder was nearly as swift [and mean] as were earlier reactions to *Brown vs. the Board of Education*. One editor of the *Yazoo Herald* informed his Yazoo City readers that "Through the furor over the Emmett Till case we hope someone gets this over to the nine ninnies who comprise the present U. S. Supreme Court. Some of the young Negro's blood is on their hands also."

Prosecutors had based much of their case on the testimony of Willie Reed, an eighteen-year-old high school student and farmhand on a plantation near Drew. Reed in his testimony at the trial claimed he saw Till, along with three whites and two blacks, in a pickup truck shortly after the kidnapping:

"The truck pulled into equipment shed near Drew, Mississippi and he heard 'licks and hollers' that sounded like a beating. The prosecutors never asked Reed to identify the other men in the truck.

Two months after the high profile trial, author William Bradford Huie somehow encouraged the slayers of Emmett Till to confess to the crime. Not only did Milam and Bryant admit to abducting Till, Milam also admitted that he shot the fourteen-year-old in the head.

Although Huie's interview was published in the January 1956 issue of *Look* magazine, Milam and Bradley could not be legally prosecuted because of the constitutional prohibition against double jeopardy. Yet even in their home community of Ruleville, Milam and Bryant were being ostracized for "disgracing" their community for their well-publicized act.

The story of Emmett Till was not destined to go away. As new accounts of Till's murder were told, some became more chilling and more intriguing than initial stories:

Professor Christopher Metress, sleuthing historical materials written by black journalists attending and covering the trial, found a story focusing on Howard Spence, a Mississippi native who had helped Medgar Evers with the investigation by watching searchers look for Till's body in the river.

In one interview, Spence remembered how "They began to search the rivers; they began to search from place to place.... And as a result [Till] was found in the Tallahatchie River. When they brought him to Greenwood, what we had formerly thought was a bullet hole – it was explained to us that it was a bit that had been drilled through the child's head. This is a fact – I'm only talking facts."

While working through back issues of the Washington Afro-American, "one of the half-dozen or so black papers that devoted extensive coverage to the case," Metress found an "open letter" dated November 19, 1955, from James Hicks to Attorney General Herbert Brownell and FBI Director J. Edgar Hoover.

Hicks, who covered the Till trial for the National News Association, was informing two government officials how to find new evidence about the murder that would allow the federal government to claim jurisdiction and open up a new prosecution of Milam and Bryant.

The journalist had provided specific directions for locating a witness, Leroy "Too Tight" Collins, who was in hiding and hard to find. He suggested agents go to "Reid's Café" and talk to cotton pickers to learn what "Too Tight" was saying about the murders:

"Listen to them tell how Too Tight boasts that the hole in the Till boy's head was not a bullet hole, but a hole drilled in his head with a brace and bit by one of the white men."

The FBI briefly considered the matter, Metress wrote, but decided not to enter the case, stating that it did not have jurisdiction because state lines had not been crossed.

Another black journalist, Louis Lomax, came into the Delta a month later searching for Loggins, the second young black who might have participated in Till's murder. Lomax told Henry he found

Loggins and that he was close to a mental breakdown. Loggins had begged Lomax not to ask questions, and then Loggins disappeared, never to be heard from again.[29]

THOUSANDS OF LETTERS protesting the Mississippi verdict poured into the White House. Mamie Till, with this new support, took her fight to the people and gave speeches to overflowing crowds across the country.

Blacks were brought together as memberships in the NAACP soared. African Americans were angered by Emmett's killing and the injustice, and moved by the loss of an only child to a young mother. In December 1955, Rosa Parks refused to give up her seat to a white passenger on a Montgomery city bus and was arrested for violating Alabama's bus segregation laws. Soon after, a 26-year-old minister, Martin Luther King Jr., called for a city-wide bus boycott. The civil rights movement was officially born.

Mamie Till Mobley died in 2003 at the age of 81. She had kept frequent contact with several Mississippians, including Drew attorney Cleve McDowell, who was born the same year as her son, Emmett, in 1941. McDowell spoke with Till's mother often, said his former office manager, Nettie Davis.

"Cleve kept many records on the Till Case. Unfortunately, they were burned up [or somehow disappeared] in a fire that happened six months after Cleve was murdered in 1997."[30]

But until her death, Till's mother always maintained that two black men, Leroy "Too Tight" Collins and Henry Lee Loggins, were with the killers that night.

The two men's names emerged in 1955 news accounts as possible prosecution witnesses who may have been jailed during the Milam/Bryant trial to prevent their testimony.

NEARLY FIFTY YEARS after the murder of Emmett Till, on May 10, 2004, the U. S. Justice Department launched a new investigation of the case to determine whether others were involved in the kidnapping and brutal slaying of young Till. Federal authorities at the time said they were acting in part "on information that materialized in a pair of documentaries focusing on the Till's death and from numerous letters urging the government to reopen the case that spurred national outrage."[31]

Alexander Acosta, assistant attorney general for civil rights, suggested that others were involved in the killing, including two black field hands. "We owe it to Emmett Till, and we owe it to ourselves, to see whether after all these years some additional measure of justice remains possible," he told *USA Today* reporters Kevin Johnson and Laura Parker.[32]

Acosta sent staff members to meet with Mississippi authorities and talk over new information about the case – new facts that were included in *The Untold Story of Emmett Louis Till,* a documentary shown to Mississippi officials that January. At the time, filmmaker Keith Beauchamp suggested that "as many as 10 people could have played a role in the murder."[33]

Stanley Nelson, director of a separate PBS documentary, *The Murder of Emmett Till*, which first aired in 2002, told the *USA Today* reporters it was "clear there were other people who have evidence who never gave it at the trial. We quickly and easily found them," Nelson said.

"I hope the Justice Department will quickly and easily find others." Acosta said FBI agents were being dispatched to assist in an investigation to be headed by an assistant district attorney in Sunflower County.

District Attorney Joyce Chiles of Greenville, said that she hopes the autopsy now will positively identify Till as well as perhaps lead to a cause of death. The ADA assigned to Sunflower County was Hallie Gail Bridges.

The disappearance of the original court transcript[34] and most courthouse documentation from the case may affect efforts to prosecute the case. In mid-May of 2005, however, the FBI announced that a "copy of the copy" of the transcript had been located in their Jackson office. Described as faint and barely legible, this would be the only publicly known record of the trial.[35]

The cotton gin fan used to weigh down Till's body when it was dumped into the river was also missing. The fan, a key piece of physical evidence, had been stored in the Sumner courthouse's basement, but disappeared when the facility was renovated in the 1970s.

"When the contractor moved in to renovate the courthouse, what the county hadn't moved out, he just threw in the street," Circuit Judge Andrew Baker said.[36]

On June 1, 2005, in Alsip, Illinois federal investigators worked to unearth a concrete vault containing Emmett Till's casket at a suburban Chicago cemetery, looking for clues into the 1955 slaying.

The muddy cement vault was loaded onto a flatbed truck and headed to the Cook County Medical Examiner's office were an autopsy was planned. There had been no previous autopsy performed when the young black Chicagoan was killed officials announced.

FBI spokesman Frank Bochte told CNN reporters at the time of the unearthing the purpose was to "positively identify the remains and dispel any rumors as to whether it is truly Emmett Till or not." A second reason was to "see if any further evidence can be looked at to help Mississippi officials bring additional charges if warranted."[37]

But as FBI and other law enforcement officials worked to find any new information, said one long-time Drew observer, "... as far as rumors go around here, the FBI has struck out in learning much of anything in Drew."

In other words, few in the small Delta community were going out of their way to offer what they might know about the case according to the woman whose own parents had secreted away Milam and Bryant in their home for 5-6 hours the night after Till's murder, helping them to hide from law enforcement officials.

"X," A BLACK DELTA businessperson grew up in nearby Minter City and was ten when Emmett Till was killed. "My mother was so worried about us. I had brothers and sisters, and she told the girls and then the boys about what happened. Sometimes we traveled to Drew and my mother was afraid for our safety."[38]

Her mother told X and her siblings that the young Chicago visitor was killed after he went into the store in Money with another boy. "She said he whistled at a dog that was sitting on a chair, and Carolyn Bryant thought Emmett was whistling at her. I don't think she believed this, herself, but she didn't want to scare us."

There were also whispers that Emmett Till was castrated before he was finally killed – "X" was told this by her mother. "We grew up with the hurt of what happened to Emmett Till. My brothers were always afraid that someone would take them away and kill them, too – just like Emmett Till."[39]

MYRLIE EVERS, widow of the slain civil rights leader Medgar Evers, later reflected on the Till murder, identifying it as "the story in microcosm of every negro in Mississippi:"

> For it was the proof that even youth was no defense against the ultimate terror, that lynching was still the final means by which white supremacy would be upheld, that whites could still murder Negroes with impunity, and that the upper- and middle-class white people of the state would uphold such killings through their police and newspapers and courts of law.
>
> It was the proof that Mississippi had no intention of changing its ways, that no Negro's life was really safe, and

that the federal government was either powerless, as it claimed, or simply unwilling to step in to erase this blot on the nation's reputation for decency and justice. It was the proof, if proof were needed, that there would be no real change in Mississippi until the rest of the country decided that change there must be and then forced it.[40]

Tribute to Rev. George Lee on the street where he was killed in Belzoni only weeks before Emmett Till was murdered.

EPILOGUE

Once the Milam-Bryant trial in Sumner ended, less than a month later in the nearby small cotton town of Glendora, a black service station attendant and father of four children was killed by a friend and co-worker of J. W. Milam's.

Elmer Kimball murdered Clinton Melton and then nineteen days later, Melton's young wife was killed in a "car accident", one week before Kimball's murder trial opened.

Clinton Melton was shot to death approximately four miles from where Emmett Till's body was dumped into the Tallahatchie River earlier in August, according to several older blacks who lived in the area at the time.

Kimball had lived in Glendora for a short time, managing a local cotton gin, and had an account at the gas station where Melton worked.

On the day of Clinton Melton's murder, Kimball, 35, was driving a car borrowed from Milam when he drove to the gas station and asked for a fill-up.

Melton's daughter, Deloris Melton Gresham, was a toddler when her parents were killed, but she later was told what occurred at the service station that day: "When Kimball drove up to the station, my father's boss told my father to go out and fill up his car. But when he was done filling the car, Kimball went into a rage and said he only wanted $1.00 of gas, and that he was going to go home and get his gun to shoot him.

"The gas station owner tried to talk him down, but couldn't. He told him my father was a good negro and that he did not deserve to be hurt. He really pleaded with Kimball – this is what I've been told.

"As soon as Kimball left, his boss said that he had better leave, fast. But my father's car was out of gas and he had to fill it first. And so Kimball came right back and began shooting at my father. Another man was in the car with Kimball, and yelled for him not to shoot. He jumped out of the car and ran into the station to hide."

Upon his arrest, Kimball claimed Melton shot at him first. McGarrh [the white owner of the gas station] denied this, adding that Melton did not have a gun at any time during the quarrel. A bullet hole was found in the windshield of Melton's parked car."[41]

The gas station in Glendora is gone, but the site of Clinton Melton's murder, where the station once stood, is still visible.

AN ANGRY HODDING Carter reacted to the murder of Clinton Melton, "one of Mississippi's own," comparing his death to the Emmett Till case in a *Delta-Times* editorial:

[Melton] was no out-of-state smart alec. He was home-grown and "highly respected.".... There was no question of an insult to Southern womanhood. There was only an argument about ... gasoline. There was no pressure by the NAACP, "credited" with the outcome of the Till trial.... So another "not guilty" verdict was written at Sumner this week. And it served to cement the opinion of the world that no matter how strong the evidence, nor how flagrant is the apparent crime, a white man cannot be convicted in Mississippi for killing a negro.[42]

Little attention was paid to the death of Delores Gresham's mother that occurred on or around December 21, 1955, approximately nineteen days after Clinton Melton was killed on December 3. Officially, her mother's death was blamed on faulty driving. "Later, a relative told me that was not true, that everyone knew she was run off the road," Gresham said.[43]

Gresham, then a toddler, still remembers the fear of being trapped inside her mother's car as it sank to the bottom of a murky bayou on the outskirts of Glendora. A relative driving by saved her life and that of her baby brother. But Beulah Melton drowned.

"My mother was a pretty woman, known for being bright and outspoken," Gresham said. "People who knew her have told me we are very much alike – both in looks and in personality."

Gresham learned that her mother had been picking up information on her husband's death and would have been a "problem" for Kimball at the trial.

From news accounts and the talk around Glendora, there was no provocation of her father's killing. It was outright murder, according to white witnesses, including the white service station owner. The Melton family was well known in Glendora. Clinton Melton had lived there all his life and, "for once, white people spoke out against the killing of a negro. The local Lions Club adopted a resolution branding the murder 'an outrage' [and pledging to donate $400 to the family]," Myrlie Evers, widow of civil rights leader Medgar Evers, later wrote in "For Us the Living."[44]

Melton's widow told Medgar Evers she feared justice would not be done if the NAACP interested itself in the case, and asked him not to become involved. "Her wishes were respected."[45] In a later investigation after her death, Medgar Evers discovered the club had given the widow only twenty-six dollars of the promised $400 and that a local white minister had given her sixty dollars of his own.

Relatives took in Delores Melton Gresham and her siblings, and Gresham continued to live in Glendora with her grandmother. "My grandfather was so upset, he left Glendora and never came back."

Unlike some earlier Mississippi white on black murders, Kimball was charged for the murder and although not convicted, he spent some time in jail:

Kimball Loses Bid for Freedom on Bond

Sumner, Miss. (AP) –December 28, 1955 – Elmer Kimball today lost his bid for freedom on bond while awaiting grand jury action on a charge of murdering a Negro man.
Three justices of the peace held a preliminary hearing for the white gin operator and refused bond. Officers returned Kimball to jail to await action of the grand jury which meets next March. The hearing was held in the little courthouse where the sensational Emmett Till trial was held. Bond usually is refused in cases where a person is accused of a crime which carries a possible death sentence upon conviction.
Kimball is charged with murder in the shotgun slaying of Clinton Melton, Negro service station attendant at nearby Glendora and father of four children. The accused man testified he fired in self-defense after someone shot at him

three times. Kimball said he didn't know who fired until he returned the fire and killed Melton.

Lee McGarrh, Melton's employer, testified that Kimball fired without provocation, and Melton was unarmed. He said Kimball became angry at the Negro during an argument over gasoline for Kimball's car. McGarrh said Kimball declared he was going home for his gun and [sic] kill Melton.[46]

One wire service sent a staff member to cover the Kimball trial, and the only Mississippi newspaper that sent a staffer was Carter's Greenville *Delta Democrat-Times*. David Halberstam was still in Mississippi after the Milam-Bryant trial and covered the trial as a freelancer.

This time cameras were barred, not only from the courtroom but also from the entire courthouse property, and no press table was set up. The sentiment [for conviction] was particularly strong in the Glendora community where Kimball shot Melton and where both the deceased and the defendant were well known. "Elsewhere in Tallahatchie County, of course, it tended to become the usual matter of a white man and a black man."[47]

Defining "Good" and "Bad"

Halberstam must have taken a dose of cynicism after observing the Milam and Bryant trial. Assessing the judicial environment beforehand, he wrote with a sense of wit, that a friend of his divides the white population of Mississippi into two categories.

> The first and largest contains the good people of Mississippi, as they are affectionately called by editorial writers, politicians, and themselves. The other group is a smaller but in

many ways more conspicuous faction called the peckerwoods.

The good people will generally agree that the peckerwoods are troublemakers, and indeed several good people have told me they joined the Citizens Councils because otherwise the peckerwoods would take over the situation entirely. It is the good people who will tell you that their town has enjoyed racial harmony for many years, while it is the peckerwoods who may confide that they know how to keep the niggers in their place; it is the good people who say and mean, "We love our nigras," and it is the peckerwoods who say and mean, "If any big buck gets in my way it'll be too damn bad."

But while the good people would not act with the rashness of and are not governed by the hatred of the peckerwood, they are reluctant to apply society's normal remedies to the peckerwood. Thus it is the peckerwoods who kill Negroes and the good people who acquit the peckerwoods; it is the peckerwoods who hang dead crows from the trees of a small town and the good people who do not cut them down.[48]

Despite his pleas of self-defense, Kimball was denied bond in two preliminary hearings. The biggest problem at the trial facing District Attorney Roy Johnson and County Attorney Hamilton Caldwell was swearing in fair and impartial jurors [from] a group "sworn by birthright to protecting the interest and life of the white."

The state produced three witnesses, the main one McGarrh, "a stern little man who is a member of one of Glendora's most respected families."[49]

McGarrh stayed with the same story he told at earlier hearings, swearing that he saw Kimball shoot the unarmed

Melton. Even under cross examination he remained unshaken. The only weakness in his story was that although Kimball had given prior warning of his intention, McGarrh stayed inside the station with his shot gun, Halberstam wrote.

The next witness, John Henry Wilson, "a Negro in whom Kimball said he had a great deal of confidence," did not witness the shooting, but he damaged the self defense theory. He was standing outside the station when Kimball returned with a gun. He asked Kimball what he was going to do." *"I'm going to kill that nigger,"* Kimball said.

…. The last witness for the state, George Woodson, said he was standing about ten feet away from the scene. He said he saw Kimball walk around the side of the station with a gun, and that he did not see any gun in Melton's hand.[50]

The defense did not have any eye witnesses and tried to shake the testimony of the state's witnesses. Its witnesses came up with only minor points, according to Halberstam. "But more significant than their testimony were their positions—a sheriff, a deputy sheriff, and a chief of police."

But it was Kimball who did the most damage to himself when he got on the stand:

[He] got up there before those twelve Mississippians and told them a story about his relations with Melton that flatly contradicts all the Mississippi mores. Kimball told how he drove up to the station, ordered gas, and then changed his mind: "'I wish you'd make up your damn mind,' Clinton told me. I told him that kind of talk would get him in trouble, and he said, 'I'm not afraid of you or any other white son of a bitch.'" Kimball said he went inside and told McGarrh that Clinton was getting pretty nasty and asked him to total up his account and he'd be back and settle up; when he returned a few minutes later someone started firing at him, hit him, and he went back to his car and got his shot gun.[51]

Halberstam asserted that Kimball's story would be hard for any jury to swallow because they would *know* that "no white peckerwood gin manager, the best friend of J. W. Milam, would let a Negro talk like that without doing a little whupping right there on the spot."[52]

After four and one-half hours, the jurors walked in and announced their decision to acquit and a Delta reporter filed this story:

> Sumner, Miss. (AP) – Elmer Otis Kimball was acquitted of murder late yesterday in the shotgun slaying of a 33-year-old Negro. "I wasn't sure justice would be done," said the 35-year-old white Glendora cotton gin operator, "but I should have known." A 12-man, all-white jury, made up mostly of farmers, deliberated more than four hours before freeing Kimball.
>
> Two witnesses testified they saw Kimball blast Clinton Melton three times with a shotgun December 3 at a Glendora service station. Witnesses said the shooting was an aftermath of an argument between Kimball and Melton over gasoline to be put into Kimball's car. Kimball testified that Melton cursed him during the argument. Defense Atty. J. W. Kellum said Kimball fired the fatal shots in self-defense. Kimball said three shots were fired at him before he opened fire, one wounding him in the shoulder. He showed a scar and brought in a doctor who verified the gunshot wound. But neither Lee McGarrh, white owner of the service station, not George Woodson, Negro, who said he

witnessed the slaying, said they saw or heard Melton fire. No weapon was found on Melton's body or in his car. The trial took place in the same courtroom where half-brothers J.W. Milam and Roy Bryant were found innocent six months ago of the murder of 14-year-old Emmett Till, Chicago Negro. Kellum was one of five defense attorneys in the Till case.[53]

Melton's murder and the acquittal of Kimball further cemented a recognition that times were becoming more dangerous for Mississippi's African Americans, if that was even possible. One white Glendora resident, asked by a visiting reporter for his opinion of both the Till and Melton murders told him, "There's open season on the Negroes now. They've got no protection, and any peckerwood who wants can go out and shoot himself one."[54]

CLINTON AND BEULAH MELTON'S daughter never moved from the Delta. She kept a picture of her mother who looks like she could be her twin. While she has never owned a picture of her father, Gresham said she would have liked to know him better. She continued to question what happened to her mother on that frightening day, as well.

And her story had a happy note. In 2003, a New York filmmaker accidentally discovered a copy of an old newsreel showing the story of Clinton Melton's murder and became intrigued. The filmmaker incorporated the reel into a documentary on Emmett Till, and made sure that Gresham had a copy for her family. The following year, the documentary was shown on a Chicago television station, resulting quite by chance in one of Gresham's brothers discovering his lost sister. A family reunion took place that summer. "It was joyous," Delores Gresham said. "We talk to each other on the phone several times a week, and I'm meeting other relatives through my brother."

TILL'S SADISTIC MURDER and the easy release of his killers (followed by the Melton murder) made it again clear, at least for some, that change had to come. On December 1, after the Milam-Bryant trial had ended, Rosa Parks refused to surrender her seat to a white person on a segregated Montgomery, Alabama, city bus. On this same day Mississippi's U. S. Senator James O. Eastland announced that desegregation was dead.

Parks later became a friend of Till's mother and once told Mamie Till-Mobley she was thinking about a good many things on that important day, but she was thinking about Emmett Till, as well, "and she couldn't be moved."

Journalist Bill Minor was one of the first journalists to acknowledge this important relationship between the Till murder and Rosa Parks' decision. At the time, Minor was a 35-year-old reporter who had been covering Mississippi for the *New Orleans Times-Picayune* for almost nine years. He later wrote of "seeing the historic significance of the Sumner courtroom when Milam and Bryant were acquitted."[55]

National media attention surrounding Emmett Till's death, the trial, and the inevitable acquittal of his killers had an effect that no one could have imagined or predicted, Minor wrote, becoming "a key factor in the explosive year that launched the modern Civil Rights Movement."

At the end of the trial, Minor wrote and filed a dispatch stating, "To the sweaty, tense courtroom audience, it was clear that not two men but a system as old as the Constitution of the United States, and a way of life which may be older, had been on trial."

Parks' courageous act of civil disobedience led to the Montgomery Bus Boycott and the entrance of a young minister, Dr. Martin Luther King, Jr., as a powerful leader in the fight for civil rights. Emmett Till's lynching had galvanized Black leaders and ordinary citizens, including Parks.

A few years later, when four students from North Carolina Agricultural and Technical University (A&T) integrated the Woolworth's lunch counter in Greensboro – starting a movement across the South – they, too were affected by Emmett Till's lynching. Several told PBS interviewers years later they had felt depressed by it, leading them to talk to others about how things should be.[56]

* * *

SEVERAL EVENTS occurred in Mississippi shortly around the time of the death of Emmett Till that would hamper democracy and ensure that little would improve in the Magnolia state for many years. In the wake of the May 1954 *Brown v. Board of Education* ruling[57] 101 Southern Senators and Congressmen on March 12, 1956, introduced a "Southern Manifesto," written by Senator Eastland, a wealthy Sunflower County planter and white supremacist.

The decree rejected the U.S. Supreme Court's school integration decision and pledged to use "all lawful means to bring about a reversal of this decision which is contrary to the Constitution and to prevent the use of force in its implementation."

Mississippi legislators took another step on March 29 voting 129 - 2 for a bill sponsored by House Speaker Walter Sillers to create the Mississippi Sovereignty Commission "to fight integration." Gov. J. P. Coleman signed the bill into law eight days later, and as governor, sat as the first chair of the commission.

Mississippi had responded to *Brown* with legislation to shore up the walls of racial separation. The act creating the Commission provided the agency with broad powers. The Commission's objective was to "do and perform any and all acts deemed necessary and proper to protect the sovereignty of the state of Mississippi, and her sister states . . ." from perceived "encroachment thereon by the Federal Government or any branch, department or agency thereof." To exercise this loosely define objective, the Commission was granted extensive investigative powers.[58]

Under Governor Ross Barnett more spies were hired to watch individuals and organizations that challenged the racial status quo. Commission investigators snooped throughout the state, gossiping with law enforcement, private white Citizens Councils members, school administrators, bankers, lawyers and others to compile reports on civil rights activities in the counties, often labeling black citizens and northern civil rights volunteers as "communists." Investigators also responded to specific requests from local state officials and members of the public for spy-collected information, including license plate numbers, phone numbers and addresses of those in the civil rights movement.

The Sovereignty Commission also relied on informants, paying them from a few dollars to cover expenses to regular monthly sums of $500. The Commission employed private detectives; most investigators came from military and FBI backgrounds.

Through the Sovereignty Commission flowed public funding for the [private] white Citizens' Councils that were formed shortly after Brown in 1954 to control African Americans by running them out of town or engaging the Ku Klux Klan's services to make their harassment more permanent. If a black person tried to send their child to a "white" school, Counselors might ensure their business was ruined or their house shot into. Citizens Councils still operate, according to founder Tut Patterson.

Until December 1964, the Commission documented monthly grants of citizens tax dollars given to the white Citizens' Councils amounting to hundreds of thousands of dollars. Since thousands of files were hidden or even demolished, other money transfers may never be known. (Former Commission director Erle Johnston in his autobiography bragged that some Sovereignty Commission files would never see the light of day.)[59]

The Sovereignty Commission also participated in the national campaign to prevent the passage of the 1964 Civil Rights Act, establishing and moving funds for the Coordinating Committee for

Fundamental American Freedoms or CCFAF under the direction of Yazoo City attorney, John Satterfield (twice past president of the American Bar Association).

It is not that difficult to document that most of the money – millions of dollars – used to support the state's racist campaign against the Act along with the building of private segregated "academies," came through the Sovereignty Commission, Citizens Councils and CCFAF but originated via the foundation of a rich old white supremacist from New York City, Wycliffe Draper. The money trail is found in some of the Commission's records that survived Johnston's purge and in a book, Scientific Racism, by Dr. Bill Tucker of Rutgers University.

Johnston eventually called for removal of all "incriminating" reports, especially those indicating the Commission helped county registrars stop African-Americans from registering to vote. He also described the investigative work of the Commission as "preventative medicine" to avoid "bad situations," and asserted that the Commission was "not a super snooping agency trying to crack down on any Negro who raises his hand."

Investigators continued to track individuals and groups who challenged racial segregation, although the subjects of investigations were referred to now by the more generic anticommunist term "subversives" rather than the earlier brand "race agitators." The Commission also continued its advisory function, primarily advising how to circumvent civil rights legislation.[60]

Eventually the Sovereignty Commission folded. Some say that another spy agency, the Mississippi Bureau of Investigation, served as its replacement. Regardless, the rest is history – preserved history, at that.

Through the efforts of several Mississippians and the American Civil Liberties Union, the modern civil rights years in Mississippi remain a fascinating period of time to study, with many details uniquely conserved by the state of Mississippi's Department of

Historical Archives with "secret" spy records available for public consumption on the Internet ... even if it wasn't planned to happen that way.[61]

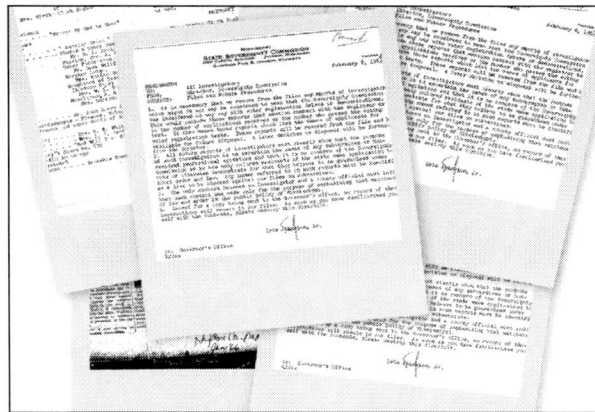

Historical Sovereignty Commission documents.

SOME THIRTY YEARS after reporting on the Emmett Till case for Ebony magazine, Cloyte Murdock Larsson, a former Ebony staffer, returned to the Mississippi Delta to observe *The New Mississippi*.[62]

The Emmett Till trial coverage she initially provided was still in her mind. Larsson and young Till had shared the same birth date. "There are some stories that a journalist can never forget no matter how hard one tries. Like fading pictures in a photo album, certain impressions remain in the mind long after time has erased the details of the events. For me, the Emmett Till murder case was that kind of assignment."

After the trial was over, Larsson worked abroad for the next thirty years, returning to the United states in 1986 to write the thirty-year anniversary story for *Ebony*.

Larsson had joined the team of writers and photographers from Johnson Publishing Company who volunteered to cover the trial and when the all-white jury returned an acquittal, she saw "a side of the American way of life that even I, a Southerner, found shocking. Prejudice was a phenomenon that I was prepared for …but not open, raw, vulgar menacing hate."

One day before the trial began, *Ebony* and *Jet* photographer David Jackson and Larsson visited Rev. Moses Wright at his weathered gray tenant farmhouse in Money. Larsson recalled, "While we sat talking on the porch, an open truck came rumbling down the road. It slowed as it approached the house, and in my mind's eye I can still see the six white men standing in the back, armed with shotguns that glittered in the sun.

"How slowly the truck seemed to move…so slowly that I could see the eyes of the men regarding us with a cold and ageless hostility. The menace was obvious, the message clear. The spell was not broken until, abruptly, the truck picked up speed and raced on."

Laarson met Sheriff Strider, "another unforgettable Mississippian," the following day at the courthouse in Sumner. "Standing in the entrance to the courtroom, like the anointed defender of the unreconstructed South, he rested his right hand meaningfully on his gun as he saw the members of the Black press approach.

"Malevolently aware that we could do nothing except accept his insult, swallow our rage and go on, [Strider] said with a poisonous smile, 'Mawnin', niggers!'"

Larsson got the message. "We were behind enemy lines now. We had no rights that a White man was bound to respect. Our press cards were no guarantee of safety. Not even a member of the U. S. Congress could expect a courteous welcome, not if he happened to be both Northern and Black. Congressman Charles Diggs of Michigan discovered that quickly enough when he joined us to witness the proceedings. "A nigger congressman!" scoffed a white deputy at the door. "It ain't possible. It ain't even legal!"

Knowing that any encounters with white journalists would arouse suspicion, Larsson and the other black reporters on their team were careful to pretend they did not know the white photographer who had come with them to photograph "aspects of the trial and of Mississippi life which it would have been impossible for Black reporters to cover." They would only meet secretly with Mike Shea to exchange information quickly at pre-arranged rendezvous points.

Since the telephones in the homes of Black activists were tapped, Larsson dared not use them to make contact. "We could have exposed our White companion and drawn unnecessary attention to our hosts, militant Blacks of Mississippi who were already in trouble enough. Dr. T. R. M. Howard, with whom some of us stayed in Mound Bayou, had received many death threats. For his family's protection and ours during the Till trial, he kept a small arsenal of shotguns behind the door."

Most spectators at the Till trial were white Mississippians, not to Larsson's surprise. Some brought their children and their box lunches. "They bought soft drinks from vendors who curtly refused to sell their wares to Blacks, and peered admiringly at Carolyn Bryant, the 'victim' of the alleged wolf whistle."

When Sheriff Strider told the court that the body which he had pulled out of the water had deteriorated to such an extent that "he couldn't be sure whether it was that of a Black person or a White," Larsson's temper flared.

And then she did something out of character: "During a pause in the trial, I pushed my way through the milling crowd of Whites and asked Judge Curtis Swango, whose impressively evenhanded conduct of the trial was like a breath of fresh air, why, if Sheriff Strider was unsure of the victims racial identity, he had asked a Black undertaker to take charge of the body!"

Heads turned. Eyes focused on Larsson, and.... "I felt like a marked woman. The White Citizen's Councils were active in the area. I had seen a letter on White Citizens' Council stationery on Sheriff George Smith's desk when David and I had visited his office. I knew that a White reporter from the North had been run out of town, and I knew that Sheriff Strider was perhaps the last man in Mississippi whose truthfulness I should publicly challenge."

As the trial proceeded, the courtroom tension was so high that when someone dropped a glass bottle – it shattered – the sound was like a shot. "In a single, reflex reaction, everybody, Blacks and Whites alike, ducked."

After the acquittal, Larsson remembered she was dismayed. It had seemed clear from evidence presented that a strong case had been made against the accused. "Till may or may not have wolf whistled. What did it matter? He had a right to life. I thought about his last moments, the terror...the blows...the bullet. How could anyone have done such a thing to a 14-year-old child?"

On their return trip to Sunflower and Tallahatchie counties, the news team tried to interview Roy Bryant at his present place of business, a country-style general store in Ruleville. Bryant granted them an interview, but did not say much. He told Larsson the case had hurt him, financially and that after the trial, his customers in Money found other places to shop.

"Forced to give up the business, he left Mississippi, and his wife Carolyn eventually left him. His half-brother, J. W. Milam, also moved out of state and, like Roy, split up with his wife," Larsson would learn.

Larsson found that Milam had died from cancer. Sheriff Strider was dead and so was Moses Wright, whose house in Money had been leveled. "I remember him as a brave man whose finger never shook when, in that hostile courtroom, he pointed out Milam and Bryant."

What in the past would have been a quiet lynching had made news around the world and Larsson on her trip back to the Mississippi Delta found some whites were still embarrassed. She traveled to Clarksdale to interview Aaron Henry who by then was serving a second term in the state legislature. Henry had been one of the NAACP officials who had helped produce the "missing witness" that the FBI may never have found.

Henry told Larsson that white men had been killing black boys in the Delta for years without ramifications. But this time, perhaps "the hand of God" was involved, causing the Emmett Till case to become a cog in the wheel of change. "Perhaps we have television to thank for that," Henry told Larsson.

Searching for Roy Bryant, Larsson and her team met up with attorney Cleve McDowell in a courtroom in Clarksdale of Coahoma County. McDowell took them to see Bryant during a quick trip around the counties.

The black attorney who was the regional director of the NAACP in his state looked vaguely familiar to Larssan. "We had seen his picture in the newspapers. In 1963, he was the first Black student, after James Meredith, to be admitted to the University of Mississippi and the first ever to study law there. After the murder of NAACP Field Secretary Medgar Evers, McDowell learned that he and James Meredith were next in line for assassination. McDowell bought a gun. 'Most everybody else had one," he said, 'but when mine was discovered, I was expelled.'"

McDowell finished his education at the Thurgood Marshall School of Law in Texas, a "better and safer" place to be. The black law school was emphasizing civil rights law and the University of Mississippi was far behind, he would later tell oral history interviewer, Owen Brooks.

Larsson was surprised that Bryant's store was in a black Ruleville neighborhood. But McDowell explained that Bryant wasn't worried "because blacks forget" and that "even when they know what certain whites have done, they don't do anything about it."

But this was no reason to think the Klan had gone away, McDowell reminded her. "They're not wearing sheets any longer.

They're wearing gray flannel suits! But some of them have just gone under cover. And some of them are doing it to us in a different way— the Northern way. If Northern whites had been in power down here, we'd still be in slavery!.... Now, we have situations like Black lawyers being harassed by the bar association, and we have economic freeze- outs whenever big money is involved."

A young Cleve McDowell attends The "Ole Miss" law school.

In McDowell's opinion, conditions in some places were worse in 1986 than in 1955: "You can see open sewers, a level of poverty as bad as in some deprived, developing countries, with insects crawling over everything. Down here, we've still got a massive job to do."

McDowell introduced Larssan to Greenwood Councilman David Jordan and his wife, Christine, both science teachers in Greenwood's integrated city schools. Both had fought long and hard for civil rights and as president of the Greenwood Voters' League for 20 years, Jordan was instrumental in initiating lawsuits aimed at democratizing the political and educational systems.

The Jordans were at the movie theater in Greenwood when Emmett Till's body was pulled out of the Tallahatchie River and Jordan remembered feeling shocked that someone in their midst could kill a 14-year-old child.

"After that happened, we were ready to do whatever was necessary to change the social conditions which had made this possible."

DURING THE REST of the Decade, the Emmett Till case remained the overriding force in black people's minds. It was "evident that white people didn't care," the Greenwood teacher told Larssen in 1986.

"I am intelligent enough to realize that the same kinds of things that happened once could happen again...We are still in the struggle, and even though we have made some gains, we are still skeptical."

About the author

Susan Orr-Klopfer, MBA, is a writer currently living in the Yazoo Mississippi Delta at Parchman Penitentiary ("the farm") with her husband, psychologist, Fred J. Klopfer, PhD. The Klopfers live in Sunflower County between the site of Emmett Till's murder and the trial of Milam and Bryant in Sumner. They both enjoy traveling around the Delta, taking photographs and talking to older people who've lived their lives in Mississippi. Their son, Barry C. Klopfer, Esq., is an assistant district attorney in New Mexico. Both Fred and Barry assisted with writing *Where Rebels Roost, Mississippi Civil Rights Revisited*, available June 25, 2005.

Author's Note: *The Emmett Till Book* is comprised of excerpts from *Where Rebels Roost —Mississippi Civil Rights Revisited* (LULU Press, publication date June 25, 2005,) and is nonfiction. Descriptions and dialogue are based on interviews conducted with eyewitnesses and participants in the events described. In addition, newspapers, books, journal and magazine accounts were used. Other resources were documents, letters, diaries, and oral histories from various libraries, archives and private collections.

Two other primary sources used were government materials provided under the provisions of the Freedom of Information Act and material from the archives of the Mississippi Sovereignty Commission, available online.

Appendix

The small town of Drew, Mississippi in Sunflower County has a long history of white on black violence. There are many untold stories that will never surface, but townspeople still talk about the murders of Joe Pullen, Jo Etha Collier, and Cleve McDowell – occurring in 1923, 1971 and 1997, respectively. This Appendix covers each of these murders and also provides an *Emmett Till Timeline* and an *Emmett Till Who's Who List*.

I. Emmett Till Timeline

1955

May 7: The Reverend George Lee, a grocery owner and NAACP field worker in Belzoni, Mississippi, is shot and killed at point blank range while driving in his car. Citizens Council ("uptown Klan") involvement is suspected. Several weeks later in Brookhaven, Mississippi, Lamar Smith, another black man, is shot and killed in front of the county courthouse in broad daylight and before witnesses, after he voted. Both men had been active in voter registration drives. No arrests were made in connection with either the Lee or Smith murder. The murders of Lee were identified by the FBI many years later, but no charges were filed against the two men, both Belzoni residents.

August 19: A day before her son leaves for a summer stay with Mississippi relatives, Mamie Till gives fourteen-year-old Emmett the ring that was once owned by his father Louis Till inscribed with the initials L.T.

August 20: Mamie Till takes Emmett to the 63rd Street station in Chicago to catch the southbound train to Money, Mississippi, a cotton hamlet in Tallahatchie County.

August 21: Emmett Till arrives in Money, Mississippi, and goes to stay at the home of his great uncle Moses Wright.

August 24: Emmett joins a group of teenagers to go to Bryant's Grocery and Meat Market for cool refreshments after a long day of picking cotton in the Delta sun. Bryant's Grocery, owned by a white couple, Roy and Carolyn Bryant, sells supplies and candy mostly to black sharecroppers and their children. Emmett goes into the store to buy bubble gum. Some of the kids report Emmett whistles at Carolyn Bryant and/or makes a smart alec remark to her.

August 28: About 2:30 a.m., Roy Bryant, and his half brother J. W. Milam, kidnap Emmett Till from Moses Wright's home and take him to a machine shed on a plantation outside of Drew in Sunflower County. They later describe to a national magazine reporter of brutally beating him, taking him to the edge of the Tallahatchie River, shooting him in the head, fastening a large metal fan used for ginning cotton to his neck with barbed wire, and pushing the body into the river. The two men return to Glendora to "wash off the blood" at a friend's home. Afterwards, they head out for Ruleville to spend the next night in the home of Bryant's relatives by marriage.

August 29: J. W. Milam and Roy Bryant are arrested on kidnapping charges in Leflore County in connection with Till's disappearance. They are jailed in Greenwood where they are held without bond.

August 31: After three days, Emmett Till's decomposed corpse is pulled from the Tallahatchie River, several miles upstream from Money, between Glendora and Phillip. Moses Wright identifies the body from a ring with the initials L.T. The body is moved from Greenwood to Tutwiler for embalming before it is sent by train to Chicago.

September 1: Mississippi Governor Hugh White orders local officials to "fully prosecute" Milam and Bryant in the Till case and appoints a former FBI agent to assist the prosecutor.

September 2: Mamie Till arrives at the Illinois Central Terminal to receive her son's casket. She is surrounded by family and photographers who snap her photo collapsing in grief. The body is taken to the A. A. Rayner & Sons Funeral Home.

A Jackson newspaper condemns the "brutal, senseless crime" but complains that the NAACP is working "to arouse hatred and fear" by calling Till's murder a lynching.

September 3: Emmett Till's body is taken to Chicago's Roberts Temple Church of God for viewing and funeral services. The casket is kept open as thousands of Chicagoans wait in line to see Emmett's brutally beaten body.

September 6: Emmett Till is buried at Burr Oak Cemetery. The same day, a grand jury in Mississippi indicts Milam and Bryant for the kidnapping and murder of Emmett Till. They both plead innocent and are held in jail until the start of the trial in Sumner, Tallahatchie County's "second" seat of government, even though the alleged murder occurred in nearby Sunflower County.

September 15: *Jet* magazine, the nationwide black magazine owned by Chicago-based Johnson Publications, publishes photographs of Till's mutilated corpse, shocking many people from coast to coast.

September 17: The black newspaper *The Chicago Defender* also publishes photographs of Till's corpse.

September 19: The kidnapping and murder trial of J. W. Milam and Roy Bryant opens in Sumner with jury selection; blacks and white women are banned from serving on the all-white, 12-man jury.

Selected are nine farmers, two carpenters and one insurance agent. Mamie Till Bradley departs from Chicago's Midway Airport to attend the trial. She will spend each night at the home of Dr. T. R. M. Howard of Mound Bayou.

September 20: Judge Curtis Swango recesses the court to allow more witnesses to be found. NAACP leaders and black and white reporters team up to locate sharecroppers who reportedly saw Milam's truck and overheard Emmett being beaten.

September 21: Moses Wright, Emmett Till's great uncle, bravely accuses two white men in open court. While on the witness stand, he stands up and points his finger at Milam and Bryant, and accuses them of kidnapping Emmett from his home.

September 23: Following jury deliberation of 67 minutes, Milam and Bryant are found not guilty of murdering Emmett Till. One juror reports that they wouldn't have taken so long if they hadn't stopped to drink pop. Roy Bryant and J. W. Milam are photographed as they light up cigars and kiss their wives in celebration of the acquittal.

Moses Wright and another poor black Mississippian who testified, Willie Reed, are smuggled to Chicago. Once there, Reed collapses and mentally suffers.

September 26: Some European newspapers term the acquittal "a judicial scandal in the United States." *Le Drapeau Rouge* (the Red Flag) publishes: "Killing a black person isn't a crime in the home of the Yankees: The white killers of young Emmett Till are acquitted!"

September 30: Milam and Bryant are released on bond with kidnapping charges pending.

October 15: *The Memphis Commercial Appeal* publishes an article reporting that Louis Till was executed by the U.S. Army in Italy in

1945 for raping two Italian women and killing a third after Mississippi Senator James O. Eastland leaks the "information" to the press.

October 22: The American Jewish Committee in New York urges Congress to toughen Federal civil rights legislation in a report that includes quotes from newspapers in six European countries expressing outrage after the Till verdict

November 9: Moses Wright and Willie Reed testify before a LeFlore County grand jury in Greenwood, Mississippi. The white men refuse to indict Milam or Bryant for kidnapping and the two white men go free.

December 5: One hundred days after Emmett Till's murder, Rosa Parks refuses to give up her seat on a city bus, launching the Montgomery, Alabama bus boycott and the modern civil rights movement.

1956

January 24: *Look* magazine publishes an article written by William Bradford Huie, entitled *The Shocking Story of Approved Killing in Mississippi*. Huie offers Roy Bryant and J. W. Milam $4,000 to tell how they killed Emmett Till. Milam speaks for the record.

1957

January 22: William Bradford Huie writes another article for *Look* magazine, "What's Happened to the Emmett Till Killers?" Huie writes that "Milam does not regret the killing, though it has brought him nothing but trouble." Blacks have stopped frequenting stores owned by the Milam and Bryant families and put them out of business. Bryant takes up welding for income, and both men are ostracized by the white community.

1980

December: J. W. Milam dies in Mississippi of cancer.

1990

September: Roy Bryant dies in Mississippi of cancer.

1997

Drew attorney, Cleve McDowell, is murdered in his home under suspicious circumstances. McDowell, born in the same summer as Emmett Till, had maintained frequent contact with Emmett's mother over the years. All of his research files on the case were reportedly burned in a fire six months after his murder.

2003

January 6: Mamie Till Mobley dies of heart failure, at age 81. Her death comes two weeks before a documentary, *The Murder of Emmett Till*, is to premiere nationally on PBS.

2004

May 10, the U. S. Justice Department launches a new investigation of the case to determine whether others were involved in the kidnapping and brutal slaying of the young man.

2005

June 1, Federal investigators unearth a concrete vault containing Emmett Till's casket at a suburban Chicago cemetery, hoping to find clues into his 1955 slaying.

II. Emmett Till Who's Who

This page was last updated on June 19, 2005. I have listed people with the names they had at the time of the Emmett Till murder and trial. http://emmetttillmurder.com.

Abbey, Richard Huntington "R. H." (1891-1986) was a member of the 18-man Tallahatchie County grand jury that handed down indictments of murder and kidnapping against J. W. Milam and Roy Bryant on September 6, 1955. He married Mary Ellen McCormick in 1925.

Adams, Olive Arnold (?-) was the author of an investigative work titled *Time Bomb: Mississippi Exposed and the Full Story of Emmett Till*, published within two weeks of the article in *Look* that featured the confessions of J. W. Milam and Roy Bryant. Adams's work differed drastically from that piece. She was the wife of Julius J. Adams, publisher of the *New York Age Defender*.

Allison, Lee Russell (c. 1916-?) lived in Glendora, Leflore County, Mississippi, and was one of the character witnesses for J. W. Milam in the Milam-Bryant murder trial. He married Verda Louise Coleman in 1940.

Armstrong, Howard (1919-1993) served on the jury in the Milam-Bryant murder trial. At the time of the trial, he was a farmer living in Enid, Tallahatchie County, Mississippi. He married Jane Helms in 1942 in Charleston, Tallahatchie County.

Bell, Charles (?-?) was a member of the 18-man Tallahatchie County grand jury that handed down indictments of murder and kidnapping against J. W. Milam and Roy Bryant on September 6, 1955.

Billingsley, Walter (c. 1923-?) was slated as a witness for the prosecution in the Milam-Bryant murder trial, but was not called to testify. He was a milkman on the Sheridan Plantation near Drew, Sunflower County, Mississippi, and witnessed the sounds of the beating in the barn on the morning after Emmett Till was kidnapped in Money. This plantation was managed my Leslie Milam, brother of J. W. Milam and half brother to Roy Bryant

Black, Herbert "H. T." (1914-1988) was a member of the 18-man Tallahatchie County grand jury that handed down indictments of murder and kidnapping against J. W. Milam and Roy Bryant on September 6, 1955. He served as a corporal in the U. S. Army during World War II.

Black, Joseph (1925-1976) was a member of the 18-man Tallahatchie County grand jury that handed down indictments of murder and kidnapping against J. W. Milam and Roy Bryant on September 6, 1955. He served as a staff sergeant in the U. S. Air Force during World War II.

Booker, Simeon (?-) has been a correspondent for *Jet* magazine since 1953. He covered the Milam-Bryant murder trial for that publication and soon after published his "Negro Reporter at the Till Trial" in the *Nieman Reports*. He had earlier won the Harvard Nieman Fellowship and then became the first black reporter to work for the *Washington Post*. He was also the first Black to win the National Press Club's Fourth Estate Award.

Boyce, L. W. (?-?) lived in Glendora, Leflore County, Mississippi, and was one of the character witnesses for J. W. Milam in the Milam-Bryant murder trial.

Bradley, Amanda (c.1905-?) lived on the Sheridan Plantation near Drew, Sunflower County, Mississippi at the time of the Emmett Till murder. This plantation was managed my Leslie Milam, brother of J. W. Milam and half brother to Roy Bryant. As one of the surprise witnesses gathered by the prosecution, she testified at the murder trial that she saw four white men entering and exiting a barn on the plantation the morning after Emmett was abducted. She also saw a truck outside of the barn. After the trial she, like other of the black witnesses, was moved from Mississippi to Chicago.

Bradley, Mamie Elizabeth Carthan Till (1921-2003) was the mother of Emmett Louis Till. She was born to Wiley Nash and Alma Smith Carthan in Webb, Tallahatchie County, Mississippi. When she was two years old, the family migrated north to Argo, Cook County, Illinois, a racially mixed community near Chicago. From 1936 to 1941 she was employed as a domestic worker; from 1941-1943 she worked for the Coffey School of Aeronautics, and from 1953 to 1956 she was employed by the Federal Government, in charge of confidential Air Force files. She married Louis Till in 1940 and gave birth to her only son, Emmett, in 1941. She and Louis later separated but were never divorced. Louis, later serving in the army in Italy, was executed in 1945. Mamie married Pink Bradley on May 5, 1951. They too divorced. On June 24, 1957, she married Gennie Mobley. In 1956 she entered the Chicago Teacher's College, where she graduated Cum Laude in 1960. She taught in Chicago schools until her retirement in 1983. During her years as a teacher, she earned a master's degree in Administration and Supervision at Loyola University. In 1973, she trained the first group of children, who would become the Emmett Till Players, to recite speeches of Dr. Martin Luther King, Jr. She continued to speak and push for justice in her son's slaying up until the time of her death, during which time she served as president of the Emmett Till Foundation. She also co-authored a play with David Barr, *The State of Mississippi vs Emmett Till* which was performed in such cities as Chicago, Los Angeles and San Diego from 1999 to 2001. She also co-authored her own memoirs with Christopher Benson, *Death of Innocence: The Hate Crime That Changed America*, published soon after her death in 2003.

Breeland, Jesse Josiah "J. J." (1888-1969) was one of five defense attorneys representing Roy Bryant and J. W. Milam in their murder trial. He was a graduate of Princeton University and began to practice law in Sumner, Tallahatchie County, Mississippi in 1915. He married Sue H. Savage in 1917 in Sumner. He later went on to become Tallahatchie County chairman of the Republican Party.

Bryant, Carolyn Holloway (1934-) was born in Indianola, Sunflower County, Mississippi. She won two beauty contests in high school, and at age 17, left school to marry Roy Bryant on April 25, 1951. She was the victim of the alleged "wolf whistle" by Emmett Till while she was running the counter at the Bryant Grocery and Meat Market on August 25, 1955 in Money, Leflore County. She testified during the murder trial that on the occasion of the whistle, "a Negro man" had grabbed her and asked her for a date. Judge Curtis Swango decided that her court testimony was not admissible before the jury. She had born two sons with Roy Bryant by the time of the trial, and later had a third. The store in Money closed soon after the murder trial, and the family later moved to Texas. They returned to Mississippi in 1972. In 1979, she and Roy Bryant divorced, and she has since remarried three times. One husband was Billy Wilson, but she is now known as Carolyn Donham. She lives in Greenville, Washington County, Mississippi, and has refused all requests to discuss the case. She is currently under investigation by the FBI as a possible accomplice in the kidnapping and murder of Emmett Till.

Bryant, Roy (1931-1994) was one of the accused killers of Emmett Till. He was born a twin in Charleston, Tallahatchie County, Mississippi to Henry and Eula Morgan Milam Bryant. He attended the Baptist church in Charleston as a child, and for a time lived in Tutwiler, Tallahatchie County. He later spent three years in the military as a paratrooper (1950-53). He married Carolyn Holloway on April 25, 1951, and the couple had three sons. Bryant also had a daughter before his marriage to Carolyn. After the murder trial, due to black boycotting of his store, he was forced to close the business. Around this time he and J. W. Milam sold their story confessing to the murder of Emmett Till, to reporter William Bradford Huie for $3,500, and it was published in *Look* magazine. In 1956 he went to the Bell Machine Shop in Iverness, Mississippi, and learned welding with the help of the G. I. Bill. He worked as a welder and boilermaker for 16 years in East Texas and Louisiana. He and his family then moved to Ruleville, Sunflower County, Mississippi, in 1973, and Bryant lived there until his death. Legally blind as a result of his years as a welder, he came to own another general store in Ruleville, which he ran until it burned down in 1989. As in Money three decades earlier, the store catered mainly to a black clientele. He and Carolyn divorced in 1979 and he married Vera Joe Orman in 1980. In 1983, while running his grocery store, he was indicted for buying food stamps for less than their value and then selling them at full price to the government. He plead guilty to two counts of food stamp fraud, but due to the pleas of his attorney, he was sentenced to only three years probation and a $750.00 fine. Four years later, however, he was again charged with food stamp fraud and was sentenced to two years in prison. However, he was released after only eight months. In neither conviction, was his involvement in the Till case discussed in the court, and both times, he received the minimum sentence because his attorney argued for leniency, as Bryant had been "a good citizen." Toward the end of his life he spent most of his time at home, but sold watermelon and other fruit at a stand along the road in Ruleville in the summertime. Plagued with health problems, he nearly lost his feet due to diabetes and eventually died of cancer at the Baptist Hospital in Jackson, Mississippi.

Caldwell, James Hamilton, Jr. (1898-1962) was one of three members of the prosecuting team representing the state of Mississippi at the Milam-Bryant murder trial. He was married to Sarah Petterson, and at the time of the trial he was recovering from a heart attack and was unable to bear much of the responsibility of the prosecution team. He had initially opposed the grand jury indictment, stating his belief that "the case was lost from the start." Unfortunately, he drowned seven years after the trial.

Caldwell, N. T. (?-?) was a member of the 18-man Tallahatchie County grand jury that handed down indictments of murder and kidnapping against J. W. Milam and Roy Bryant on September 6, 1955.

Campbell, Maybelle (?-?) was Emmett Till's school teacher at McCosh Elementary School in Chicago, and spoke at his funeral on September 3, 1955. She called him "a fine upstanding pupil."

Carey, Archibald (1908-1981) was a former Chicago alderman and preacher who spoke at the Emmett Till funeral.

Carlton, Caleb Sidney (1915-1966) was one of five defense attorneys representing Roy Bryant and J. W. Milam. He was admitted to the bar in 1939 and began practicing law in Sumner, Mississippi in 1945. He later became president of the Mississippi Bar Association.

Carter, Hodding (1907-1972) was a journalist who covered the Milam-Bryant murder trial for the *Delta-Democrat Times*, which he founded by merger in 1938. He remained with the paper as editor and publisher until the mid 1960s. He received a B.A. from Bowdoin College in 1927 and did graduate work in journalism at Columbia University. He was awarded a Neiman Fellowship at Harvard in 1940 and later that year helped found the daily *PM*. During WWI, he served in the Mississippi National Guard. He was a progressive journalist and known as the "Spokesman for the New South." In 1946 he won a Pulitzer Prize for his editorials against segregation and racist injustice, and was censured in 1955 by the Mississippi legislature for his criticisms of the White Citizens Councils. He was the author of numerous books

Carthan, Wiley Nash "John" (1902-1969) was the father of Mamie Till-Mobley and grandfather of Emmett Till. He was born in Mississippi and lived there until moving to Argo, Cook County, Illinois with his wife and daughter in 1924. He worked for Corn Products in Argo until his divorce from Alma Smith Carthan in 1932. He moved to Detroit, Michigan and remarried. His relationship with Mamie was an estranged one until she and Emmett moved briefly to Detroit and in with the Carthans. He accompanied Mamie to the murder trial in Mississippi in August 1955, providing emotional support during that difficult week. He died at the home of his brother Emmett Carthan while visiting his relatives in Argo and Chicago. He went by John Carthan at the time of the trial.

Chancellor, John (1927-1996) was a journalist who covered the Milam-Bryant murder trial as a national reporter for NBC. Two years later, also reported on the desegregation of Central High in Little Rock, Arkansas. He came to NBC in 1950 after two years with the *Chicago Sun-Times* and worked as a correspondent on the *Huntley-*

Brinkley Report. He became host of the *Today Show* in 1961 and later served as director of Voice of America from 1965-1967. He became head anchor on the *NBC Nightly News* from 1970 until his retirement in 1982. He was the sole anchor for most of his tenure.

Chatham, Gerald (1906-1956) was the district attorney who prosecuted J. W. Milam and Roy Bryant in their murder trial. He had practiced law in the district since 1931. He had also served as a state representative, county superintendent of education, and county prosecuting attorney before he was elected district attorney in 1942. He held that office until 1956. Unfortunately, he died at home of a heart attack a year after the trial in Sumner, an event his family blames on stress related to the case.

Cole, Gwin (?-) was an identification officer for the Mississippi Highway Patrol. He was one of the investigators appointed by governor Hugh White to Drew, Sunflower County, Mississippi to examine the shed on the Sheridan plantation where, according to witnesses, Emmett Till was alleged to have been beaten. When questioned about his role in this investigation recently, Cole had no recollection of the case.

Coleman, James Plemon "J. P." (1914-1991) was Mississippi Governor Elect at the time of the Milam-Bryant murder trial and assigned his own special agent, Robert Smith, to aid the prosecution. Prior to his election as governor, he had been an aid to a U. S. congressman, and served as district attorney, circuit judge, state attorney general, and justice of the Mississippi Supreme Court. As governor, he was successful in maintaining racial segregation in Mississippi. After his term as governor ended, he was elected to the state House of Representatives. He ran for governor again in 1963 but lost. In 1965 he was appointed to the United State's Fifth Circuit

Court of Appeals and held the rank as chief judge from 1979 to
1981. He retired from the fifth circuit in 1984.

Collins, Levy "Too Tight" (1923-1993) has been tied to the
murder of Emmett Till by various witnesses. At the time of the
murder, he was employed by J. W. Milam, and was allegedly in the
truck the morning Emmett was taken to the Sheridan plantation near
Drew, Sunflower County, Mississippi. Investigators learned that to
prevent him from witnessing in court, Sheriff H. C. Strider placed
him in jail elsewhere in Tallahatchie County under a false name. In
an interview published in the *Chicago Defender* shortly after the trial, he
denied any involvement with the murder. Later in life, he was
working in a cotton compress warehouse in Drew and died there of
natural causes.

Cothran, John Ed (c. 1915-) was deputy sheriff to Leflore County
sheriff George Smith. He arrested J. W. Milam on charges of
kidnapping Emmett Till and was a witness for the prosecution at the
Milam-Bryant murder trial. He later served as sheriff of LeFlore
County from 1960-1964.

Crawford, John (1933-) was one of several youths who was with
Emmett Till in the evening before his kidnapping. He is the brother
of Roosevelt Crawford and uncle of Ruth Crawford, two of the local
teenagers who witnessed the incident at the Bryant Grocery and
Meat Market. He currently lives in Detroit, Michigan.

Crawford, Roosevelt (1939-) was one of several youths with
Emmett Till who went to Bryant's Grocery and Meat Market on
August 25, 1995, when the incident between Emmett and Carolyn
Bryant occurred. He maintains that Till did not whistle at Bryant but
that he was responding to a bad move made by a checker player on
the porch. He is the brother of John Crawford and uncle of Ruth

Crawford, both of whom were also present. He currently lives in Detroit, Michigan.

Crawford, Ruth Mae (?-) was one of several youths with Emmett Till who went to Bryant's Grocery and Meat Market on August 25, 1995, when the incident between Emmett and Carolyn Bryant occurred. Speaking publicly for the first time in Keith Beauchamp's film *The Untold Story of Emmett Louis Till*, she says she watched Till through a window and that all he did to upset Bryant while in the store was place his money in her hand, rather than on the counter. She is the niece of Roosevelt Crawford, who was also present that evening, and John Crawford.

Daley, Richard J. (1902-1976) was the mayor of Chicago at the time of the Emmett Till murder, and spoke out publicly against the killing. He sent a telegram to President Dwight D. Eisenhower asking that "all the facilities of the federal government be immediately utilized so that the ends of justice may be served." His tenure as mayor began in 1955 and ended with his death twenty-one years later. He attended DePaul University and graduated with a degree in law in 1934, but because of his immediate election to the Illinois state legislature, he never practiced. In 1968 he hosted the Democratic National Convention.

Desmond, William (?-?) was a journalist who covered the Milam-Bryant murder trial for the *New York Daily News*.

Devaney, Ed (1881-1957) served on the jury in the Milam-Bryant murder trial. At 74, he was the oldest member of the jury. He lived in Charleston, Tallahatchie County, Mississippi, and was a retired carpenter.

Diggs, Charles, Jr. (1922-1998) was the African-American congressman from Michigan who attended the Milam-Bryant murder trial. He worked in his family mortuary business before being elected to the Michigan state senate in 1951. He was later elected to the U. S. House of Representatives in 1955 and served until resigning in 1980. In 1978 he was charged with diverting $60,000 in office operating funds to pay his own expenses. He was convicted and served seven months in prison. Despite his conviction, he was re-elected to his office. He did appeal his conviction, but was censured by the House and stripped of his committee membership before his resignation. After leaving congress, he opened a funeral home in Maryland and earned a degree in political science.

Dogan, Harry H. (1895-?) was Tallahatchie County sheriff-elect at the time of the Milam-Bryant murder trial. He served from 1956-1960. He allegedly helped pick jurors for the trial that would likely favor an acquittal of the accused. According to one of the defense attorneys, Dogan sent word to the jurors while they were deliberating to stall the verdict in order to make it "look good."

Duke, Grover (1924-1982) lived in Money, Leflore County, Mississippi, and was one of the character witnesses for Roy Bryant in the Milam-Bryant murder trial.

Dyess, Claude Vernon "C. V." (1923-1965) was a member of the 18-man Tallahatchie County grand jury that handed down indictments of murder and kidnapping against J. W. Milam and Roy Bryant on September 6, 1955. He was a in the fighter control squad in World War II.

Evers, Medgar (1925-1963) was field secretary for the Mississippi chapter of the NAACP at the time of the Emmett Till murder. He, with other NAACP officials, helped to seek out witnesses for the trial. He was inducted into the army in 1943 and served in Normandy. He attended Alcorn College (now Alcorn University), where he met his wife to be, Myrlie Beasley. The two were married on December 24, 1951. The following semester, he graduated with a degree in business administration. They moved to Mound Bayou, where he worked as an insurance agent until 1954, and was active in the NAACP and in civil rights activities. He applied for, and was denied entrance into the University of Mississippi Law School. He moved his family to Jackson, where he and Myrlie set up the office of the NAACP and began investigations into violent crimes perpetrated against blacks. His work to bring down segregation made him many enemies, and late in the evening on June 12, 1963, he was gunned down in his driveway as he returned home. His killer, Byron De La Beckwith, was tried twice in 1964 and set free due to two hung juries. Beckwith was finally convicted in 1994 and died in prison.

Falls, Jerry (1905-1979) was the foreman of the 18-man Tallahatchie county grand jury that handed down indictments of murder and kidnapping against J. W. Milam and Roy Bryant on September 6, 1955. He married Elizabeth Garner in 1934 and was one of the wealthiest men in Tallahatchie County, described as "a Delta aristocrat steeped in the tradition of noblesse oblige."

Fedric, E. C. (?-?) was a member of the 18-man Tallahatchie County grand jury that handed down indictments of murder and kidnapping against J. W. Milam and Roy Bryant on September 6, 1955.

Ford, Louis Henry (1914-1995) was the bishop who preached Emmett Till's funeral sermon. He was also the presiding bishop of the Church of God in Christ and the namesake of the Bishop Ford Freeway in Chicago. He began his ministry in 1926, and became national director of public relations for the Church of God in Christ in 1945. He was elevated to the position of assistant presiding bishop in 1972 and in 1990, became presiding bishop. A graduate of Saints College in Lexington. Mississippi, he moved to Chicago in 1933. In 1963 he founded the St. Paul Church of God in Christ, and later the C. H. Mason and William Roberts Bible Institute for Bible Studies.

Fraiser, John, Jr. (?-?) was a Leflore County prosecutor who worked on the kidnapping case against J. W. Milam and Roy Bryant, as that crime occurred in that county.

Gunter, John (?-?) was a journalist who covered the Milam-Bryant murder trial for the *Memphis Commercial Appeal*.

Halberstam, David (1934-) is a journalist who covered the Milam-Bryant murder trial for the *West Point Daily Times Leader* while a reporter living in Mississippi. A 1955 graduate of Harvard, he later worked for the *Nashville Tennesseean* from 1956 to 1960, and as a *New York Times* staff writer from 1960 to 1967. In 1964 he shared the Pulitzer Prize and George Polk award for foreign reporting. In 1967 he became a contributing reporter for *Harpers*. He has authored several books, including *The Fifties* (1993), which details the Emmett Till case.

Hall, Robert F. (1906-1993) covered the Milam-Bryant murder trial for the Communist *Daily Worker*. He began his career in journalism at age 11 as a cub reporter and printer's assistant for the *Mobile Register* and the *Mobile News Item*. He worked for several newspapers before entering the University of Alabama, which he attended for one year. He later enrolled at Columbia University during the Great Depression. At this time, he sought an alternative to Capitalism, and joined the Communist Party and became editor of their student paper, *The Student Review*. He joined the *Daily Worker* in 1945 and left in 1956 due the revelations about Stalin's atrocities during World War II. He moved to New York that year and became a member of the Republican Party. He became editor of the *Valley News*, and later began publishing his own *Warrensburg News*. In 1962 he founded *Adirondack Life Magazine*. In 1969 he was appointed by Governor Nelson Rockefeller to serve on the Temporary Study Commission on the Future of the Adirondacks, and a year later was appointed the editor of *The Conservationist*. He published three books of essays, and was active in civil and community organizations.

Havens, Willie D. (1904-1998) served as the alternate juror in the Milam-Bryant murder trial. He married Mamie Glover in Charleston, Talhahatchie County in 1929. As an alternate, he was dismissed from the jury by Judge Curtis Swango before they retired to the jury room to deliberate. He was a carpenter living in Charleston.

Haynes, Goldie (1913-1989) was an evangelist who sang a solo, "I Don't Know Why I Have to Cry Sometimes," at the Emmett Till funeral.

Henderson, Robert Harvey (1921-) was one of five defense attorneys representing J. W. Milam and Roy Bryant in their murder trial. At 34, he was the youngest of the legal team. He had been a life-long resident of Tallahatchie County and had been in practice since 1947. As of 2005, he is still practicing law in Sumner, Mississippi.

Henry, Aaron E. (1922-1997) was a NAACP official at the time of the Emmett Till murder, and helped find witnesses willing to talk by disguising himself as a sharecropper and going into the fields. He served as president of the Mississippi Conference of Branches of the NAACP from 1960 to 1993, was president of the Council of Federated Organizations, Mississippi, from 1962-1965, and a member of the Mississippi House of Representatives from 1980 to 1995. He was also a pharmacist and ran his own pharmacy in Clarksdale, Mississippi.

Herbers, John (1923-) is a journalist who covered the Milam-Bryant murder trial for United Press International. He graduated from Emory University in 1949, and began his career at the Greenwood, Mississippi *Morning Star*, and the Jackson, Mississippi *Daily News*. He was a reporter for UPI from 1953-1963. He joined the *New York Times* in 1963, was appointed assistant national editor in 1975, deputy Washington bureau chief in 1977, and Washington national correspondent in 1979. He retired n 1987. He has authored several books, including *The Lost Priority: What Happened to the Civil Right's Movement in America?* (1970).

Hicks, James L. (1915-1986) was a reporter who covered the Milam-Bryant murder trial. His investigation into the murder was published in several installments in the *Baltimore Afro-American*, the *Cleveland Call and Post*, and the *Atlanta Daily World*, soon after the trial. He began his career in journalism in 1935 with the *Call and Post*. He joined the army and was awarded three battle stars for his service in the New Guinea campaign, and was promoted to captain. After World War II, he joined the *Afro American* in Baltimore and became the Washington Bureau Chief for the National Negro Press Association. He served as editor for the *Amsterdam News* from 1955 to 1966, and again from 1972 to 1977. He was the first African American member of the State Department Correspondents Association and the first African American accredited to cover the United Nations. In 1977 he became editor of the *New York Voice*.

Hodges, Robert (c. 1938-) was the young fisherman who discovered Emmett Till's body in the Tallahatchie River at a spot called Pecan Point, near Philipp, on August 31, 1955. He was a witness for the prosecution at the murder trial.

Holland, George (1913-1982) served as a juror in the Milam-Bryant murder trial. He was a farmer living in Glendora, Tallahatchie County, Mississippi.

Howard, Theodore Roosevelt Mason "T. R. M." (1908-1976) was a doctor, entrepreneur, and fraternal leader in the all-black town of Mound Bayou in the Mississippi Delta. He was chief surgeon of the Friendship Clinic and owned an insurance company, home construction firm, a large plantation, and many other investments. In 1951, Howard founded the Regional Council of Negro Leadership, a civil rights and pro-self-help organization that sponsored an annual rally/festival/speech in Mound Bayou. Speakers at this event included Thurgood Marshall and Rep. Charles Diggs. Medgar Evers, who moved to Mound Bayou to sell insurance for Dr. Howard, was an early leader of the RCNL. During the Milam-Bryant murder trial, Dr. Howard searched for witnesses and other evidence to secure a conviction as well as to prove a broader conspiracy. Mamie Bradley stayed in Dr. Howard's house during the trial, as did many black reporters.

Hubbard, Joe Willie (?-?) was alleged by T.R.M. Howard to have been an accomplice of J. W. Milam and Roy Bryant in the murder of Emmett Till. This claim was also put forth by two other writers who published investigative pieces on the murder in 1956: Olive Arnold Adams in *Time Bomb: Mississippi Exposed and the Full Story of Emmett Till*, and Amos Dixon (pseudonym) in a series of articles in the *California Eagle* (although Adams uses the pseudonym "Herbert" for Hubbard). Although Willie Reed and Henry Loggins recently recalled having once known Hubbard, no one knows what happened to him.

Huff, William Henry (1888-1963) was a NAACP attorney who represented Mamie Bradley after Emmett Till was murdered. He later terminated his services with her when the NAACP ended its sponsorship of Mrs. Bradley's speaking tour. He attended Georgia Normal and Industrial Institute and Knox Institute in Athens, Georgia. He also attended the Chicago Law School, obtaining his L.L.B., and and the John Marshall Law School for his J.D. He was admitted to the Indiana Bar in 1936 and the Illinois Bar in 1946. He was also admitted to practice before the U.S. Supreme Court. In addition to law, he was trained at the National Medical University in Chicago, and practiced pharmacy.

Huie, William Bradford (1910-1986) was the reporter who paid J. W. Milam and Roy Bryant $3,500 to tell their story after their acquittal. Their confession appeared in an article by Huie in *Look* magazine in 1956. He graduated from the University of Alabama in 1930 and worked as a reporter for the *Birmingham Post* from 1932-1936, and as associate editor for *American Mercury* from 1941-1943. He served in the U. S. Navy from 1943-1945, and then returned to the *Mercury* as editor and publisher until 1952. In the 1950s, he interviewed political figures for the CBS series, *Chronoscope*. He authored numerous books over the years, including the 1959 *Wolf Whistle*, a chapter of which deals with the Emmett Till murder.

Hurley, Ruby (?-?) was southeastern director of the NAACP who, with Amzie Moore and Medgar Evers, helped seek out witnesses for the prosecution in the Milam-Bryant murder trial. To do so, she disguised herself as a field worker. In 1951 she had moved from New York to Birmingham to establish the first permanent office of the NAACP in the deep south. She was the first professional civil rights worker in the south.

Jackson, David (1922-1966) covered the Milam-Bryant murder trial as a photographer for *Ebony* and *Jet* magazine. He took the famous photo of Emmett Till on the slab at the A. A. Raynor & Sons Funeral Home, published in *Jet*, which shocked the nation. Just before the trial, while interviewing Mose Wright at his home, with Clotye Murdock, he witnessed a truck carrying six armed white men slow past the house.

Jones, Curtis (c. 1938-) was a cousin of Emmett Till. He traveled from Illinois to Mississippi to spend time with Mose Wright's family shortly after Emmett and Wheeler Parker had left, and was in the Wright home the night Emmett was abducted. He is quoted in the film *Eyes on the Prize* as having been at the store at the time of the incident between Emmett Till and Carolyn Bryant, although he had not yet arrived in Mississippi. He is a veteran of the Chicago Police Department.

Jones, Willie Mae Wright (c.1917-?) was the oldest child of Moses and Lucinda Larry Wright. She was the mother of Curtis Jones, cousin of Emmett Till who traveled from Illinois to Mississippi shortly after Emmett and Wheeler Parker left, and was in the Wright home the night Emmett was abducted. It was her phone call on Sunday morning, August 28, 1955, that notified Mamie Bradley that Emmett has been kidnapped from her father's home.

Kellum, Joseph W. (1911-1996) was one of five defense attorneys representing J. W. Milam and Roy Bryant in their murder trial. He had lived in Tallahatchie County since 1920 and was admitted to the bar in 1939. In 1955 he ran for District Attorney and lost that race just a week before Emmett Till was murdered.

Kempton, Murray (1917-1997) covered the Milam-Bryant murder trial for the *New York Post*. He was educated at Johns Hopkins

University, where he was editor of the *Johns Hopkins News-Letter*. He graduated in 1939 and then worked as a labor organizer until joining the *Post*. During the 1960s he became editor of the *New Republic*, and began writing columns for *Newsday* in 1981, which he did until his death. He won the Pulitzer Prize for these columns in 1985. He also authored several books.

Kilgallen, James (1888-1982) covered the Milam-Bryant murder trial for INS. He was the father of Dorothy Killgallen, a regular contestant on the T. V. game show, *What's My Line?*. He was best known for his coverage of the Lingburgh baby kidnapping, as well as the trials of Bruno Hauptman and Machine Gun Kelley.

King, Joe J. (?-?) was a member of the 18-man Tallahatchie County grand jury that handed down indictments of murder and kidnapping against J. W. Milam and Roy Bryant on September 6, 1955.

Kinnard, Roy (?-?) was a member of the 18-man Tallahatchie County grand jury that handed down indictments of murder and kidnapping against J. W. Milam and Roy Bryant on September 6, 1955.

Lance, Frank (1931-1981) was a member of the 18-man Tallahatchie County grand jury that handed down indictments of murder and kidnapping against J. W. Milam and Roy Bryant on September 6, 1955.

Loggins, Henry Lee (c. 1927-) has long been thought to be an accomplice with J. W. Milam and Roy Bryant in the murder of Emmett Till. He was employed by J. W. Milam at the time of the murder and witnesses said they saw him in the truck with Emmett Till the morning after he was abducted. Investigators learned that he was placed in jail during the trial by Sheriff H. C. Strider under a false name. He recently denied having anything to do with the murder but is under investigation by the FBI.

McCool, N. L. (?-?) was a deputy sheriff in Leflore County who aided in the kidnap and murder investigation of Emmett Till.

McGaa, Peter (?-?) lived in Glendora, Leflore County, Mississippi, and was one of the
character witnesses for J. W. Milam in the Milam-Bryant murder trial.

Malone, Harry D. (1920-1993) worked for white and black funeral homes in Tutlwiler, Mississippi at the time of the Emmett Till murder. As the embalmer of the body at the Avent funeral home in Tutwiler, MS, he testified at the trial in behalf of the defense. His testimony stated that he believed the body had been in the river for at least ten days, aiding the defense argument that the body was not that of Emmett Till.

Matthews, Bishop G. (1909-1973) served as a juror in the Milam-Bryant murder trial. He married Mildred Arlene Cole in 1937 and was a carpenter living in Charleston, Tallahatchie County, Mississippi.

Melton, Garland (1907-1962) was deputy sheriff of Tallahatchie County who arrived at the scene at the Tallahatchie Rivier where Emmett Till's body was found. He and Robert Hodges (who discovered the body) took separate boats into the river in order to retrieve the body. He married Myrtha Campbell in 1939 in Charleston, Tallahatchie County.

Milam, John William "J. W." (1919-1980) was one of the accused murderers of Emmett Till. He was born in Charleston, Tallahatchie County, Mississippi, to William Leslie and Eula Morgan Milam. He married Juanita Thompson on December 11, 1949 in Tallahatchie County, Mississippi, and they had two sons. He possessed only a ninth grade education and fought in Europe during World War II. While in the military he won a purple heart, a silver star, and other medals. Soon after the trial and acquittal, he and Roy Bryant sold their story confessing to the murder of Emmett Till to reporter William Bradford Huie for $3,500, and it was published in *Look* magazine. By 1956, Milam found he was unable to rent land and was refused a loan due to his notoriety. The Milam's moved to Texas for several years, and later returned to Mississippi. They moved to Greenville, Washington County, Mississippi in 1965. She and J. W were said to have later divorced, but he is listed as married to Juanita in his obituary, and there is no divorce record for them in Greenville or Washington County. He had worked as a heavy equipment operator in Greenville, and was retired at the time of his death from cancer.

Milam, Juanita Thompson (c. 1929-) married John W. Milam on December 11, 1949 in Tallahatchie County, Mississippi. She was at the Bryant Grocery and Meat Market when the incident between Emmett Till and Carolyn Bryant occurred, and was a witness for the defense at the trial. She and J. W. Milam were the parents of two sons and the family moved to east Texas in 1962. They later returned to Mississippi around 1965 and lived in Greenville, Washington County. She and J. W were said to have later divorced, but she is listed as his wife in his obituary, and there is no divorce record for them in Greenville or Washington County.

Milam, Leslie F. (1925-1974) was born in Tallahatchie County, Mississippi to William Leslie and Eula Morgan Milam. He was the brother of J. W. Milam and half brother to Roy Bryant, accused murderers of Emmett Till. He married Francis Moody Waldrup in 1949. According to witnesses, Emmett Till was beaten and shot in a tool shed at the Sheridan plantation that Leslie Milam managed. He may have been one of the white men present.

Miller, Chester A. (1903-1986) owned the Century Burial Association in Greenwood, Mississippi, which received Emmett Till's body after its discovery in the Tallahatchie River. He made initial preparations of the body by placing it in a casket, while law officials planned a burial in Money, Mississippi. He testified at the murder trial on behalf of the prosecution, testifying to the condition of the body as it was pulled from the river and placed in a boat. He had been called to the scene of discovery by Sheriff H. C. Strider.

Mims, Benjamin L. "B. L." (1925-2001) was in the boat with Garland Melton when Emmett Till's body was pulled from the Tallahatchie River on August 31, 1955. He married Carol Dyanne Gregg in 1950 and lived in Philipp, Tallahatchie County, Mississippi. He served as a witness for the prosecution and testified to the condition of Emmett's body at the scence.

Minyard, R.W. (?-?) was a member of the 18-man Tallahatchie County grand jury that handed down indictments of murder and kidnapping against J. W. Milam and Roy Bryant on September 6, 1955.

Mobley, Gennie (1923-2000) married Mamie Till Bradley two years after Emmett Till's death, and had several children from a previous marriage. He was a barber in Chicago when he met Mamie, and during their courtship grew close to Emmett. He accompanied Mamie Bradley to the A. A. Rayner funeral home where she examined the body for identification purposes. Gene aided in this effort as he recognized the haircut that he had given Emmett two weeks prior. He later became a well-respected Cadillac salesman in

Chicago. He traveled the country with his wife whenever she spoke on her son's case and remained her greatest supporter until his death.

Moore, Amzie (1912-1982) was a NAACP official in Mississippi who attended the Milam-Bryant murder trial and helped find witnesses for the prosecution. He worked for the U. S. Post Office in Cleveland, Mississippi from 1935 until his retirement in 1968. In 1940 he organized a rally of 10,000 Blacks in Cleveland while helping to organize the Regional Council of Negro Leadership. He took a leave from his post office duties and served for three and a half years in the military during World War II. While in the military, he joined the NAACP. After his release from the military, he opened up a gas station, beauty shop, and grocery store. During his years as a civil rights activist in Mississippi, he worked hard for the rights of African Americans to vote, and his house became a "safe house" for activists during the voter registration drives of the 1960s.

Mooty, Rayfield (1907-1990) was a cousin by marriage to Mamie Till-Mobley who traveled to Mississippi with her and her father, Wiley Carthan, for the Milam-Bryant murder trial. Through his contacts with labor organizations, he helped arrange speaking engagements for Mamie, before and after the trial.

Mullen, Claude (1907-1990) was a member of the 18-man Tallahatchie County grand jury that handed down indictments of murder and kidnapping against J. W. Milam and Roy Bryant on September 6, 1955.

Murdock, Clotye (? -) reported on the Milam-Bryant murder trial for *Ebony* magazine. Soon after the trial, she moved to Sweden and remained there until visiting Mississippi upon the 30th anniversary of the Emmett Till slaying. She published two articles in *Ebony* related to the Emmett Till case, "Land of the Till Murder," in 1956, and

"Land of the Till Murder Revisited," in 1986. Just before the trial, while interviewing Mose Wright at his home, with *Ebony* and *Jet* photographer David Jackson, she witnessed a truck carrying six armed white men slow past the house.

Murff, R. E. (?-?) was a member of the 18-man Tallahatchie County grand jury that handed down indictments of murder and kidnapping against J. W. Milam and Roy Bryant on September 6, 1955.

Nelson, Charles M. "Chick" (1908 -1990) was the mayor of Tutwiler, Tallahatchie County, Mississippi, whose funeral home embalmed and prepared Emmett Till's body for shipment back to Chicago. He served as a witness for the defense at the murder trial.

Newson, Moses (? -) is a journalist who covered the Milam-Bryant murder trial. He accompanied Ruby Hurley onto plantations where potential witnesses were working in order to warn them and bring them to T.R.M. Howard's house in Mound Bayou. Moses, like Hurley, dressed as a sharecropper.

Newton, A. C. (?-?) was a member of the 18-man Tallahatchie County grand jury that handed down indictments of murder and kidnapping against J. W. Milam and Roy Bryant on September 6, 1955.

Newton, Davis (1918-?) served as a juror in the Milam-Bryant murder trial. He was a farmer living in Enid, Tallahatchie County, Mississippi.

Otken, Luther "L. B." (1889-1969) was a physician living in Greenwood, Mississippi who testified at the Milam-Bryant murder trial on behalf of the defense. Although he only viewed the body at a distance because of the odor, his testimony as to its condition aided the defense in their argument that the body had been in the river longer than Emmett Till had been missing. He also testified at the grand jury hearing that handed down the murder indictment against J. W. Milam and Roy Bryant. He began practicing medicine in Greenwood in 1915.

Parker, Thelton (?-?) was one of the local youths who was with Emmett Till in Money, Mississippi the evening of the incident between Emmett Till and Carolyn Bryant at Bryant's Grocery and Meat Market.

Parker, Wheeler (c.1939-) was a cousin of Emmett Till who accompanied him to Mississippi from Chicago to visit relatives. He was with Emmett at the Bryant Grocery and Meat Market the night that Emmett allegedly whistled at Carolyn Bryant. He was in the home of Moses and Elizabeth Wright the night that Emmett was abducted. He was born in Mississippi and moved with his parents and two siblings to Argo, Illinois in 1947. As an adult, he worked as a barber, and became a minister in 1977. In 1993, be became pastor of the Argo Temple Church of God in Christ, the church Alma Spearman, Emmett's grandmother, helped to found.

Pennington, James Green (1918-1994) served as a juror in the Milam-Bryant murder trial. He was a farmer living in Webb, Tallahatchie County, Mississippi. He married Marinee Thomas in 1949.

Perry, Harold (1925-1977) lived in Money, Leflore County, Mississippi, and was one of the
character witnesses for Roy Bryant in the Milam-Bryant murder trial.

Popham, John (1910-1999) covered the Milam-Bryant murder trial for the *New York Times*, where he was its first southern correspondent. He worked for that paper for twenty-five years, leaving in 1958. In 1956, under his direction, the *Times* published a 50,000 word, eight-page report on the implications of racial integration in the wake of the Brown v. Board of Education decision. After leaving the *New York Times*, he later edited the *Chattanooga Times* for twenty years. After his retirement, he commuted hundreds of miles each week, from Chattanooga to Atlanta, to attend the John Marshall Law School. He earned his law degree at age 72.

Porteous, Clark (1910-1997) covered the Milam-Bryant murder trial for the *Memphis Press-Scimitar*, where he worked for forty-seven years. He also fought in World War II. From 1981 to 1988 he edited the *Collierville Herald*, and afterward became associate editor.

Price, Lee L. (1888-1985) served on the jury in the Milam-Bryant murder trial. He was married to Katherine Oldham and was an insurance salesman living in Charleston, Tallahatchie County, Mississippi.

Primm, Howard Thomas (1904-1995) was bishop of the African Methodist Episcopal Church in Louisiana at the time of the Emmett Till murder. After the body was found, he asked that September 8 and 9 be declared days of mourning, and called on all Mississippians to take part by wearing a black strip of ribbon, three inches long.

Ramsey, Augustus "Gus" (1907-1962) served as a juror in the Milam-Bryant murder trial. He was a farmer living in Enid, Tallahatchie County, Mississippi.

Ratcliffe, Robert M. (?-?) covered the Milam-Bryant murder trial for the *Pittsburgh Courier*, and was a black reporter in the confidence of Dr. T.R.M Howard.

Rayner, Ahmed A., Sr. (1893-1989) was the funeral director who received Emmett Till's body after its arrival in Chicago on September 2, 1955. He defied orders from Mississippi to keep the casket sealed and allowed Mamie Bradley to examine the remains of her son.

Reed, Add (1879-1977) was one of the surprise witnesses at the Milam-Bryant murder trial, who testified that the morning after Emmett was abducted, he walked past the barn and saw Leslie Milam and another white man. He was the grandfather of Willie Reed, who also testified.

Reed, Willie (c. 1937-) was one of the surprise witnesses at the Milam-Bryant murder trial. He lived next door to the Sheridan plantation managed by Leslie Milam and testified that he heard beating and yelling coming from a tool shed near the barn on the plantation. He also saw J. W. Milam leave the shed and get a drink of water. After the acquittal, he moved to Chicago, where, upon his arrival, suffered a nervous breakdown due to the stress built up over the trial. He later married and currently works at Jackson Park Hospital in Chicago.

Roberts, Isaiah (1912-1989) was the pastor of the Robert's Temple Church of God in Argo, Illinois, and the host pastor for Emmett Till's funeral.

Robinson, W. M. (?-?) was a member of the 18-man Tallahatchie County grand jury that handed down indictments of murder and kidnapping against J. W. Milam and Roy Bryant on September 6, 1955.

Sanders, James (?-?) lived in Money, Leflore County, Mississippi, and was one of the character witnesses for Roy Bryant in the Milam-Bryant murder trial.

Sanders, Stanny (?-?) of Indianola, Leflore County, was a district prosecutor who worked on the kidnapping case against J. W. Milam and Roy Bryant. He later served on the defense team during the 1964 murder trials of Byron De La Beckwith, accused killer of civil rights leader Medgar Evers.

Selby, Ben (1911-1985) was a deputy sheriff in Tallahatchie County who aided in the courthouse at the time of the Emmett Till murder trial. He is seen in many photographs performing a weapons search on spectators and journalists who entered the courtroom.

Shanks, W. A. (?-?) was part of the Leflore County, Mississippi sheriff's office and helped to investigate the kidnapping and murder of Emmett Till.

Shaw, James "J. A.", Jr. (1924-1979) served on the jury in the Milam-Bryant murder trial. He was a farmer living in Webb, Tallahatchie County, Mississippi.

Smith, Crosby (1908-1993) was an uncle to Mamie Till Mobley and brother of her mother, Alma Spearman. Through his efforts, Emmett Till's body was released from the state of Mississippi after attempts were made to bury it in Money. He accompanied it on the train back to Chicago. He remained a resident of Sumner after the trial, despite other's fears for his life.

Smith, Franklin (?-?) lived in Money, Leflore County, Mississippi, and was one of the character witnesses for Roy Bryant in the Milam-Bryant murder trial.

Smith, George W. (?-?) was sheriff of LeFlore County at the time of the Milam-Bryant murder trial. He arrested and booked Roy Bryant and J. W. Milam on kidnapping charges and was the one who received the initial confession of the two men that they had kidnapped Emmett Till. He testified at the trial and later at the grand jury hearing seeking an indictment on kidnapping charges. He had served as a police officer from 1935-1948, and from 1948-1952 as deputy sheriff of Leflore County. His term as sheriff lasted from 1952-1956. He ran for state representative in 1955 but lost.

Smith, Robert B., III (c. 1914-?) served on the prosecution team in the Milam-Bryant murder trial. He had served four years in the FBI before enlisting in the marines in 1944. He practiced law in Ripley, Mississippi with his uncle after his discharge.

Spearman, Alma Smith Carthan Gaines (1902-1981) was the mother of Mamie Bradley and grandmother of Emmett Till. She was born in Mississippi and married Wiley Nash Carthan in 1919. She lived in Mississippi until moving to Argo, Illinois with her husband and daughter in 1924, where she was a founder of the Argo Temple Church of God in Christ. In 1932 she and Wiley separated and divorced, after which she married Tom Gaines. He died in 1945 and she married Henry Spearman in 1947. After his death in 1967, she moved in with Mamie and Gene Mobley.

Stratten, William G. (1914-2001) was the governor of Illinois at the time of the Emmett Till murder. He called upon his attorney general, Latham Castle, to urge Mississippi authorities to make a thorough investigation of the murder. He graduated from the University of Arizona with a major in political science in 1934, and later served in the U.S. House of Representatives from 1941-43, and 1947-49. His election to the House made him the youngest person ever to serve as a U.S. Representative. He was also Illinois State Treasurer from

1943-45 and again from 1951-53. He served as the governor of Illinois from 1953-1961, the youngest person to serve in that office in the 20th century. In 1964 he was indicted on income tax charges but was tried and acquitted the following year.

Strickland, C. A. (?-?) was one of the police identification officers and served as a witness for the prosecution in the Milam-Bryant murder trial. He photographed the body as part of the inquest while it lie in Greenwood at the Centuray Burial Association.

Strider, Henry Clarence "H. C." (1904-1970) was sheriff of Tallahatchie County from 1951-1955 and was married to Wilma Burt. He was a witness for the defense at the Milam-Bryant murder trial, and his actions behind the scenes bore out his support for them. He owned a large plantation, and after the trial, five black families moved off of his land because of his actions at the trial. In 1957, he was seated in his car at a general store in Cowart, Mississippi, when a bullet was fired into the vehicle. He narrowly missed being hit in the head. In 1959, he decided to run for the sheriff's office again, but withdrew at the urging of his wife, who feared for his safety. He declined to run again in 1963 for the same reasons. From 1964 until his death, he served as a state senator for Grenada and Tallahatchie counties. In this role, he served as vice chairman and chairman of the Game and Fish Committee, member of the Public Property, Transportation, and Water and Irrigation committees, and chairman of the Penitentiaries Committee. He died of a heart attack while at a dear camp in Issaqueena County, Mississippi. Two years after his death, a portion of Mississippi Highway 32 was designated "Henry Clarence Strider Memorial Highway."

Swango, Curtis M. (1908-1968) presided as judge at the Milam-Bryant murder trial. He graduated from Millsaps College in Jackson,

Mississippi, and from the University of Mississippi law school. He was appointed to the Circuit Court bench in 1950 by then Governor Fielding Wright and was a judge of the Seventeenth Judicial District. He was praised by black and white journalists for the even-handed way he conducted the trial.

Taylor, Euclid Louise (1905-1970) was general council to the black newspaper the *Chicago Defender* and secured an interview with Levy "Too Tight" Collins, a possible accomplice in the murder of Emmett Till, once he was located after the trial. The interview, conducted over a two-day period, was published in the *Defender* on October 8, 1955.

Thomas, Travis W. (1907-1991) served as a juror in the Milam-Bryant murder trial. He married Lillie Mae Sullivan in 1928 and was a farmer living in Murfreesboro, Tallahatchie County, Mississippi.

Toole, James A., Jr. (1911-1979) served as a juror in the Milam-Bryant murder trial. He married Janie Lee McCullen in Charleston, Tallahatchie County in 1932, and was a farmer living in Enid, Tallahatchie County, Mississippi.

Tribble, Ray (1926-1998) served as a juror in the Emmett Till murder trail. He was a farmer living in Payne, Tallahatchie County, Mississippi.

Turner, Arnold (?-?) was a member of the 18-man Tallahatchie County grand jury that handed down indictments of murder and kidnapping against J. W. Milam and Roy Bryant on September 6, 1955.

Turner, Nannie Mitchell (1888-?) was a journalist who covered the Milam-Bryant murder trial. She was married to William Mitchell, one of the founders of the *St. Louis Argus*, a black newspaper and now the oldest continuous black business in St. Louis. When William died in 1945, she became business manager and later president-treasurer of Argus Publishing Co. She was also a columnist for the *St. Louis Post-Dispatch*, and was named First Lady of the Black Press by the National Newspaper Publishers Association.

Wakefield, Dan (1932-) covered the Milam-Bryant murder trial for *The Nation*. He graduated from Columbia College in 1955, and in addition to his years with *The Nation*, he was a contributing editor to the *Atlantic Monthly*, *G. Q.*, and *Image: A Journal of the Arts and Religion*. He has received many awards, including a Neiman Fellowship in Journalism, Bernard DeVoto Fellowship to the Bread Loaf Writers, and one from the National Endowment for the Arts. He has taught writing programs at Boston University, the University of Massachusetts, Boston, Emerson College, and the Iowa Writers Workshop. He is currently a Writer in Residence at Florida International University in Miami, and has written several novels and screenplays. He is the creator of the NBC television series *James at 15*

Weber, Ed (?-?) was a deputy sheriff in Tallahatchie County at the time of the Emmett Till murder and assisted when Till's body was discovered in the river. He and Leflore County deputy sheriff John Edd Cothran went to Mose Wright's home and brought him to the river to identify the body.

White, Hugh Lawson (1881-1965) was governor of Mississippi at the time of the Emmett Till murder. He held the office for two non-consecutive terms, 1936-1940 and 1951-1955. He was a large man and one of the wealthiest to ever hold the office in Mississippi. He was elected mayor of Columbia, Mississippi in 1926 and held that office until elected to his first term as governor. Between his two terms, he served from 1944-1948 in the Mississippi legislature. He was near the end of his second term at the time Emmett was killed He publicly spoke out against the killing, but was quick to contradict NAACP claims that the murder was a racist lynching, calling it "flat out murder." He authorized district attorney Gerald Chatham to appoint additional attorneys to help in the prosecution of the accused killers, and also appointed two Highway Patrol inspectors to help in the murder investigation.

Whitten, John W. (1919-2003) was one of five defense attorneys representing Roy Bryant and J. W. Milam in their murder trial. He was born in Tallahatchie County and began practicing law in Sumner in 1940. He served as Tallahatchie County chairman of the Democratic Party, and attorney for the board of supervisors. He was the first cousin of Jamie Whitten of the U. S. House of Representatives.

Wilkins, Roy (1901-1981) was elected executive director of the NAACP in 1955 and spoke out publicly against Mississippi and the Emmett Till slaying, polarizing many residents and officials in that state. He graduated from the University of Minnesota in 1923 and joined the staff of the weekly Kansas City *Call*. He became managing editor before joining the staff of the NAACP. From 1934-1949, he edited the *Crisis*, the official publication of the NAACP. Over the years, he testified at many congressional hearings, and conferred with Presidents Kennedy, Johnson, Nixon, Ford, and Carter. In 1977 he retired from the NAACP and penned his autobiography, *Standing Fast: The Autobiography of Roy Wilkins*, which was published after his death.

Wilson, L. Alex (1908-1960) covered the Milam-Bryant murder trial for the *Tri State Defender*. He earned a Bachelors degree at Florida A&M, and did graduate work at the University of Wisconsin and Roosevelt College in Wisconsin. He also served as a marine in World

War II. He taught and served as a principal in Florida High Schools and later turned to writing. He worked for several newspapers, including the *Norfolk Journal and Guide* in Virginia. He won the prestigious Wendell Wilkie Award for his coverage of the Korean War. After later working at the *Tri State Defender* in Memphis, he moved to Chicago to take over the editorship of the *Chicago Defender*. Unfortunately, he developed what appears to be Parkinson's Disease and died a year later.

Winters, F. B. (?-?) was a member of the 18-man Tallahatchie County grand jury that handed down indictments of murder and kidnapping against J. W. Milam and Roy Bryant on September 6, 1955.

Withers, Ernest C. (1922-) was the photographer who defied Judge Swango's orders and captured a photograph while court was in session. The photo was that of Moses Wright standing at the witness stand, identifying J. W. Milam and Roy Bryant as the men who kidnapped Emmett Till from his home. He got his start as a military photographer while serving in the South Pacific during World War II, and became a photographer by profession upon his return to Memphis after the war. He published a photo pamphlet of the Emmett Till murder case, and also photographed important events such as the Montgomery Bus Boycott and the strike of Memphis sanitation workers. At the funeral of Medgar Evers, he was beaten and arrested by a police officer. During his 60 year career, he has accumulated over five million photographs. His work has appeared in the *New York Times*, *Jet*, *Ebony*, *Newsweek*, and *Life*. In 1988 he was elected to the Black Press Hall of Fame and received an honorary doctorate from the Massachusetts College of Art.

Wright, Elizabeth Smith (1900-1970) was the wife of Moses Wright, sister of Alma Spearman, and great aunt of Emmett Till. She was present the night Emmett was abducted from her home, and offered J. W. Milam and Roy Bryant money if they would leave him alone. She left her home the night of the abduction and never returned. She moved to Chicago and remained there during the murder trial while her husband and son Simeon remained behind to testify.

Wright, Maurice (c.1939-c.1990) was one of several youths who accompanied Emmett Till to Bryant's Grocery and Meat Market on August 25, 1955 and witnessed the incident between Emmett and Carolyn Bryant. He was a son of Moses and Elizabeth Smith Wright. It is believed by some that he may have been the one who told Roy Bryant about the incident, setting off the events that led to Emmett's murder.

Wright, Moses (1892-1977) was the great-uncle of Emmett Till, who visited Chicago in August 1955 and brought Emmett and Wheeler Parker to Mississippi. He was born in Mississippi and married Lucinda Larry on December 16, 1911. After her death, he married Elizabeth Smith in 1925. Until 1949 he preached at a black church in Money, Mississippi, and also worked as a sharecropper on a plantation owned by Frederick Grover since 1936. He identified in court J. W. Milam and Roy Bryant as the men who came to his home the morning of August 28, 1955 and kidnapped Emmett Till. After the trial, he moved to Argo, Illinois, with his family and did some speaking engagements on the Emmett Till case sponsored by the NAACP. Due to his notoriety in the case, he was offered a lifetime job in a nursery in Albany, New York. However, he chose to stay in Argo, where he lived quietly after the case died down and his speaking engagements ended. He later worked by cleaning a bar after closing hours. He died in the White Oak Nursing Home in Indian Head Park, Illinois. Recall that J. W. Milam asked him how old he was on the night of the kidnapping of Emmett Till, and he said "sixty-four." Milam's response was that if Wright knew anyone there that night, he would never live to be sixty-five. Wright's obituary in August 1977 says he was 85 years old at his death, and his death record in the Social Security Death Index, as well as the 1900 U. S. Census says he was born in April 1892. If these are all correct, then he was actually 63, not 64, when Emmett Till was kidnapped.

Wright, Simeon Brown (c. 1943-) is the son of Moses and Elizabeth Smith Wright. He lived near Money Mississippi and was in the bed with Emmett Till at the time of his abduction on August 28, 1955. He left Mississippi with his family after the murder trial and was raised in Argo, Illinois. Currently he lives in Chicago. He is a pipe-fitter who worked for Reynolds Metals, Co. During the recent investigation, he has spoken out publicly many times about the need for justice in the case.

Young, Frank (c. 1896-?) was a field worker who worked with the prosecution by volunteering names to Dr. T. R. M Howard of accomplices of J. W. Milam and Roy Bryant, as well as leads to possible witnesses. It was intended that he testify on behalf of the prosecution but for whatever reason, he left the courthouse during the trial and did not testify.

III. Joe Pullen's Revolt

If we must die, let it not be like hogs: hunted and penned in an accursed spot! If we must die; oh let us nobly die...fighting back. – Claude McKay, 1921

In the cotton ginning Mecca of Drew, Mississippi, the birthplace of Archie Manning, some black elders still talk about a story passed down by their parents and relatives – a story focused on a 1923 gunfight raging into the early morning hours of December 15 when Joe Pullen, a tenant farmer and WWI veteran, settled a debt to plantation manager W.T. Saunders.

Pullen shot and killed Saunders during an argument and then Pullen's own life ended in a ditch at the edge of Drew when he was shot after an all-night gun battle.

The small town had buzzed with rumors that several dozen posse members were killed and possibly hundreds wounded before Pullen was taken down by machine gunners brought in from Clarksdale. Some Drew residents maintain that for years after the gunfight, there were many people left using canes and displaying other signs of injuries received during the gun battle.

There are several versions of the Joe Pullen story, both written and spoken. In one account, nearly one thousand white men searched the swamps around Drew to find Pullen. Then depending on the source, Pullen killed 4, 17 or 19 whites and wounded 8, 38 or 40 before he was machine gunned down. Pullen either died immediately or was dragged through the streets and then killed. Local news accounts of this event were few.

The weekly Indianola newspaper carried one small paragraph on December 20, 1923 reporting that: "J. L. Doggett of Clarksdale and Kenneth Blackwood of Drew, posse men wounded Friday by negro, Joe Pullen, are reported as improving rapidly as could be expected." Associated Press reports were more complete:

Four men lost their lives in a spectacular gun battle which raged until 1 o'clock this morning between Joe Pullen, Negro tenant farmer, and a posse of several hundred men in the swamps of the Mississippi delta near Drew. Nine other wounded three probably fatally. Pullen was finally captured when four members of the posse stormed the drainage ditch in which he was entrenched. The Negro died an hour later from bullet wounds. The trouble started when Pullen's employer came to his house to collect a debt.[63]

Some of the more interesting accounts are gleaned from the stories told by the people who were living at the time. Fannie Lou Hamer, well-known civil rights activist from Ruleville, often told others the shoot-out occurred when she was a child. Hamer said that Pullen's body was dragged into town and that people cut off body parts to keep as souvenirs. "Mississippi was a quiet place for a long time [afterwards]." While local press claimed that four white men had died "in defense of law and order," Mrs. Hamer recalled that Pullen had killed thirteen white men and wounded twenty-six others before dying.[64]

Dr. L. C. Dorsey remembered how as a young child living on a Sunflower County plantation between Ruleville and Drew she heard from her father and relatives the story of Pullen. Dorsey's father often did not receive the money due him as a sharecropper, and Dorsey believed the Pullen incident had much to do with his fear of questioning "the man."

The version she heard was that Pullen died because he stood up for his right not to be cheated out of his labor. After Pullen did not clear anything at settlement time, he made arrangements to go live with another black farmer, according to Dorsey:

When he returned to announce his plan … white folks got angry … and decided he wasn't going to move … [the man] wasn't going to let him take anything off the place. Pullen sent his family away and decided to stay with his belongings … the furnishings, the livestock, the mules that he needed to work with – and what my daddy called a mob crew, which was really what they called the Klan … [They] came to the house to take him out and either kill him or beat him up, to put him in his place. He was prepared for them. He shot several of them, killed some of them, and escaped to a ditch and got in a culvert and was able to hold them off for a long time. Eventually, some person poured gasoline in the ditch and set it on fire and he had to come out … and they killed him. And if that wasn't enough, they tied him to a car and drug him through the streets of Drew, cut off his ears, I think, or castrated him … and put it in jars in the city. But every black person knew that legend. Miss Hamer used to tell it. Everybody knew it.[65]

Pullen's family protested to the President [Calvin Coolidge] who sent an investigative team "because the man had been in the service, and that was what his family talked about, that this man had served his country and this is how he was treated. He had done nothing wrong and had been killed for trying to defend himself against the crew," Dorsey said.

Researcher Nan Woodruff[66] adds to the Pullen story that Sanders may have offered Pullen $150 to recruit families to work on the plantation, and when Pullen kept the money without providing the service, the fight began.[67] She terms Pullen's gunfight another "watershed event" much like the nearby Elaine Massacre[68] as blacks challenged the structure of white supremacy throughout the 1920s. Black people with guns had always threatened planter authority, particularly when disputes arose over crop contracts or merchant bills. Despite the threat of terror, black sharecroppers and laborers fought back when their lives were on the line, even if such actions resulted in their deaths.

Many researchers including Woodruff find that Southern black people had always carried guns for hunting and self-protection, but the frequency of armed confrontations between planters and croppers, based on the frequency of reporting, may have increased in the decade following World War I. Woodruff writes:

> … Pullen took the money and repaired his house and purchased other necessities that he believed the planter owed him for work he had performed and never been paid for. When Sanders and John Manning approached him, demanded he turn over the money, the six-foot tall Pullen shot and killed Sanders with a-.38-caliber pistol. As a posse gathered, Pullen seized his shotgun and ran for a ditch. He ambushed the posse, killing one with a shot to the face, hitting another in the head, and striking a third in the side. Although the posse used eight to ten boxes of shells in response, none of them hit Pullen.

> Posse members then poured a gallon of gasoline into the ditch and started a fire. The posse fired into the flames, but Pullen shot back, hitting another man. They brought in more gasoline while a party from Clarksdale arrived with two automatic rifles and a Browning machine gun. It took a third gallon of gas to reach Pullen. When he finally ran out, they shot and killed him. The posse then tied Pullen's feet to a car and dragged the body into Drew where people came from all over the region to view it. They also displayed Pullen's shotgun. Someone cut off his ear and placed it in a jar to be viewed along with the body.

According to freedom fighter Mrs. Fannie Lou Hamer, a child at the time, after the Pullen murder "Mississippi was a quiet place for a long time." While the newspapers claimed that four white men had died "in defense of law and order," Mrs. Hamer recalled that Pullen had killed thirteen white men and wounded twenty-six others before dying.[69]

Years later, it was still said that no black was safe during the cotton harvest, observed Clarksdale blues performer Will Stark:

> They had to work – or fight! When they come after a man to work, he had to go. For instance, Mister Hobson or Mister Clark or Mister King or Anderson or any of these people out of town wanted some hands to chop the cotton or plow, it make no difference who he was, he must go. They would go into colored people's house and git the children out who had never been worked none – schoolgirls – and make them go out and pick cotton … Of course the boss didn't do all this, the officers here in town would take um and when they got out on the plantation they had to work – or fight…. They just whipped um up. Some um I heard they whipped to death…. One bossman out here about Tutwiler … made a man work and chained his wife in bed at night to make sure they wouldn't run away.[70]

THE RULING WHITE Delta families would keep their immense social, economic and political power; the planters' bloc maintaining its supremacy or hegemony through an efficient capitalist economy rooted in black labor manipulation. Schooling and marriage built strong family alliances, and these white coalitions, much like Mafioso, expanded into local economies, from ownership and operation of cotton gins, to real estate, and banking.

Planters ran all of Mississippi. They frequently formed land companies to buy Delta properties; they held political, military, church and other bonds that established a "powerful, vertical integration" of local businesses into more powerful national bodies "such as the Standard Oil Company which dominated the American Cotton Oil Trust."[71]

The plantation bloc dominated political office holders – local, county, state, and national officials who enforced plantation regulations. Under these influences, oppression and censorship returned increasingly to pre-emancipation levels.

IV. The Murder of Jo Etha Collier

At approximately 9:45 p.m. on May 25, 1971, shortly after her high school graduation ceremony ended, Jo Etha Collier was talking to friends in front of a small grocery store in downtown Drew. As a pickup truck passed by, Collier was hit in the head and killed by gunshots coming from the truck.

The young graduate was shot to death by Wesley Parks, 25, of Memphis in a murder that "seemed to have no motive," said a sheriff's deputy. Wayne Parks, 25, of Drew, his brother, and their nephew, Allen Wilkerson, 19, of Memphis were riding in the truck and all three were arrested in nearby Cleveland within three hours of the shooting.

A 22-caliber pistol "with one bullet missing" was found in the car along with a 12-gauge Army issue riot gun and a 22-caliber automatic rifle, according to Sovereignty Commission reports.

But others disagreed with the police officer's "motiveless" assessment, including civil rights activist Fannie Lou Hamer, who said she was "convinced that Collier's death was indirectly connected with the current voter registration campaign."

Collier was not active with the voter registration campaign going on at the time, but visiting reporters were reminded by Hamer that black political activity in the Delta – where blacks outnumber whites – had "long met with a proportionate increase in random, almost casual, white harassment."

FBI records on the death of Collier, requested by this book's author in April 2004, were reported by the FBI as "destroyed" on March 16, 2004. No reason was given. Yet Sovereignty Commission records indicated that eight FBI investigators had been in Drew to gather information at the time of the shooting (leaving the question what was in those records and why were they destroyed?).

Police Chief J. D. Fleming of Drew had reported the three men "were very much under the influence of alcohol." Fleming took

Collier's two companions to Cleveland to identify the suspect. The three men offered no resistance when arrested in Cleveland, Fleming said.

It was Collier's first year at Drew High School. The "well-liked" student received the "School Spirit Award" on awards day, May 14, and was named the "Most Valuable Player in Track." Earlier the young woman was awarded a basketball jacket.

About 45 minutes before the fatal shooting, the men were seen sitting in their truck at a service station located less than a block away from the grocery store. When a black male asked for a light, "one of the occupants of the vehicle pointed a revolver at the negro male and told him 'I'll put all your G.D. lights out,' " the Sovereignty Commission investigator's report stated.

At Collier's funeral inside the Drew High School auditorium, Rev. Ralph David Abernathy, chair of the Southern Christian Leadership Conference, eulogized the young woman before an audience of approximately 2,000.

"The foes of evil have robbed us of one of our most dear and talented sisters…. How long will black people be mistreated in Mississippi? How long will black people be shot down in the Delta?" the SCLC leader asked.

Abernathy called for massive change that would come with black voter registrations to put blacks in office "… so that we can see that her living and dying was not in vain."

Drew Mayor W. O. Williford, seated on the stage during the rites, reportedly expressed surprise to a reporter at the large turnout of blacks and spoke of recent gains by Delta blacks: "If that many Negroes had gathered in one place when I first took office there surely would have been bloodshed."

The atmosphere was so peaceful that Williford sent away the highway patrolmen who were there in case of an anticipated flare up. Days earlier, the mayor had imposed an 8 p.m. until daylight curfew and called in the officers to help enforce it.

After the ceremony, the 18-year-old student, who was regarded highly by teachers and friends, was buried in the all-black section of the Drew cemetery. For his crime, the shooter reportedly spent two years in prison before he was released. In Drew, the rumor has persisted for years that another person was involved – a teacher.

V. The Murder of Cleve McDowell

On the day following Medgar Evers' murder Army personnel stationed at the Ole Miss campus were evacuated at dawn – just one week after James Meredith and a second black student, Cleve McDowell of Drew, had enrolled for the summer session without incident.

The decision to pull troops meant that twenty-one-year-old McDowell, accepted as the state's first black graduate student at a white university, would be left alone with no security once Meredith graduated and left campus. Meredith was so angered over the evacuation, he lashed out at those in charge. But all of the troops would be gone from Oxford by July 24.

Days earlier, as McDowell entered summer sessions at Ole Miss, Barnett spoke on television to restate that Mississippi "would not guarantee the safety of black students," contending that it was the responsibility of the federal government.

The governor also repeated his adamant opposition to integration: "We will oppose, on all occasions and at every opportunity … all dictatorial powers and police which seek to change our school system, our customs, our heritage, our way of life."[72]

Barnett had decided earlier he would not oppose McDowell, personally, as he had done with Meredith. But there were advance rumors that he might meet McDowell at Oxford and "try to talk him out of entering the university."

McDowell's entry to Ole Miss appeared easy at first, with no campus riots, but his world changed within five days after starting classes and then civil rights leader Medgar Evers was killed. Evers had been a hero to McDowell when he was a student at Jackson State and an NAACP volunteer. Meredith, one of Evers' closest friends, was anguished over the murder and had always believed he would be the one to take a bullet, not Evers.

Meredith blamed the murder on Southern governors and their "defiant actions," as well as "blind courts" and "prejudiced juries" for creating the atmosphere that made such killings possible.[73]

More than 20 percent of the faculty left Ole Miss after Meredith's achievement – about twice the normal turnover. One professor, Dr. Samuel F. Clark of the chemistry department, spoke of "serious loss of academic freedom to faculty and students" and the "breakdown of moral and professional responsibility on the part of the university's administrative officers."

Another professor left because of his family's mistreatment after he had invited Meredith over to his house for dinner on special occasions. One of the cruelest incidents occurred when his daughter was given a black doll with a card attached that read "Nigger Lover" during her school's Christmas party.

The school's law dean left the university, as well. Robert Farley, who once encouraged Medgar Evers to enter the law school and who tried to help McDowell, was in trouble once again for standing up for another professor's right to speak out freely.[74]

As fall term began, Cleve McDowell appeared outwardly calm. He was a handsome young man, slim, with high cheekbones and arrow straight posture. While he had simply taken over Meredith's dorm room instead of moving into another dorm, all of the other students moved off the floor, leaving him isolated.

Young Cleve McDowell was subjected daily to verbal harassment as he walked across the campus, and there were times that he was chased on campus as well. Several times during his drive between Oxford and his home in Drew, he was chased in his car by students wielding guns.

Once he was on his own, without any guards present, it took only three weeks before McDowell was kicked out of Mississippi's educational Mecca.

* * *

Cleve McDowell, born in Sunflower County on a plantation outside of Drew, on August 6, 1941, was the son of tenant farmers. Like other black Mississippi children of his time, his parents worked all year for a settlement – and "probably were lucky if [they] broke even," the Drew attorney told Owen Brooks during an oral history interview on August 11, 1995.[75]

In the McDowell household were two boys and three girls. McDowell had five other siblings from his father's former marriage, too. "Ferge" McDowell, his dad, lived to be 103 years old and was the first black person to be buried in the Drew Cemetery, at his son's insistence.

Both McDowell's father and grandmother loved to tell stories, and as a child, from them he learned some of the Delta's early history and how his family survived. "[My father] knew everybody and everything that had happened. His mother, a former slave, lived to be near 100, too. She could remember [back to the] Civil War. [Her] name was Sally McDowell and she hid in the chimney when the Yankees liberated that area. I think they were in Arkansas at the time," McDowell told oral historians. The McDowell family lived in a typical sharecropper home but young Cleve McDowell always felt there was something very special about their dwelling:

> We had newspaper on the walls that we replaced every year. It wasn't like somewhere you look out through the floor and see the ground and up through the top and see the air and all that, because we always kept it fixed up.
>
> We always kept the grass scraped out of the yard, and we had all kind of farm animals—hogs, chickens, geese, ducks, whatever. Then we really thought we were rich when we got that wallpaper that you could order and glue. We really thought we had made it then. But we lived a typical farm life.[76]

McDowell's family never went hungry since they had a garden and raised their own livestock.

> My father and mother believed [in] that…. We never went hungry … In the off season, you used to call it laid by, when you laid your crop by, we would go and chop wood. We'd have to cut firewood for the winter. And later on, they started giving us coal. You would get a little pile of coal that had to last you the whole season. And years later, into the early fifties, we got a kerosene stove, which was a big thing then.

> [We had] cows. I used to hate that. It was my job going getting the cows. You know, you send them out in the morning and you have to go get them in the evening for milking and what have you. It was typical farm life.[77]

Always there were rumors about the violence going on around them, the life they were shielded from as children. But sometimes, McDowell and his siblings "got an earful about everything from family lynching stories to various things that would happen in the community."

These were pre-Emmett Till years —"You knew about atrocities that happened to black people if somebody said the wrong thing or did the wrong thing or insulted some white person. Obviously [that] was tantamount to a death sentence, because you could be killed on the spot [for any reason]."

In nearby Drew, according to McDowell and others, there lived a notorious town marshal, Dewey Ross [Roth], "who slaughtered people at random for any number of years," "… until some time later – I'm thinking in the late forties or early fifties—he killed some white guy and then they finally sent him to Parchman. He'd killed a white doctor's son, as I recall, who came home from the military."

> At the time, you really weren't thinking civil rights…. That didn't really come into the Mississippi Delta until Emmett Till's case, and then we started hearing about things. [P]rior to that time, the Southern way of life was, whatever the white man said went, and you relied on your boss for protection. The traditional saying was that if you could stay out of the ground, he would keep you out of jail. There was supposedly safety in being on a certain person's plantation.[78]

McDowell would state that he knew he came up "at the right time, in the right place." "By '58 and '59 and '60, things were jumping." Many black junior high students, including McDowell, were strongly influenced by the Emmett Till lynching that took place only a few miles outside of Drew and also by the Little Rock school integration. Entering high school, the students were met by an excellent group of teachers, McDowell remembered: "We were getting teachers who were telling us what is supposed to be, even though they weren't necessarily out leading any parades or anything. With TV [available], we were becoming a part of the nation [as] we were getting more information."

Some of McDowell's teachers came out of Tuskegee Institute in Alabama while others were trained at Tougaloo College near Jackson. McDowell's school records show that he was a top student, with A's and B's in political science, speech, math and science classes. He was class president, editor of the school newspaper, captain of the debate team, and a member of several varsity sports teams.

Young McDowell worked diligently at debate, often winning awards. He practiced hard and on his oral history tapes, McDowell's voice sounds assured and well trained. His friends, during interviews, often mentioned that he had a "beautiful" voice with "perfect" diction.

In the summer of 1960, McDowell entered Jackson State, where he was active in the burgeoning Civil Rights Movement. It was there he met both Meredith and Evers, whose NAACP office was a block from the campus. He worked as Evers' student assistant, helping with the Freedom Riders – "I was the briefcase guy."

McDowell found his college professors were excellent: "They just told us like it is and they allowed us to catch up with the rest of the world in terms of politics and the right to vote, the need to know why we were voting and what our basic rights were and why we weren't inferior, all these things."[79]

McDowell finished his undergraduate degree in three years as an honor graduate, in spite of working part time to pay his tuition. Ranking tenth in the graduating class of 311, McDowell entered law school at the University of Mississippi, becoming the first African-American student to attend a "white" graduate school in Mississippi. A federal court order and United States Army troops aided his entrance in June of 1963. He later completed law school at the Thurgood Marshall School of Law at Texas Southwestern University in Houston, where he was President of the Student Bar Association and received several merit awards.

The young student would not have known that the state's Sovereignty Commission was looking for "anything which would reflect on his moral fitness and academic record in order to block his entry into the University of Mississippi School of Law."[80]

Investigator Tom Scarbrough visited Drew on May 29, 1963, searching for whatever he could uncover, but apparently found nothing to hold back the application. After speaking with the town's mayor, chief of police, "two white teachers," and the principal of the "Negro School," Scarbrough reported:

All of those to whom I talked in Drew, including all of the elected officials, stated … they had known the McDowell boy all of his life. All stated he had never been involved in any kind of meanness to their knowledge. The school principal reported that McDowell participated in all kinds of campus activities such as athletics and school plays, and he personally considered him above the average Negro boy in conduct; however I noted the following observations … by three different teachers who taught McDowell: N. H. Thorp, who taught social science, [wrote] that McDowell was capable of doing much better with his school work if he would apply himself.

R. E. Cox, who taught English, [wrote] "this child should watch his over-anxious attitude as it could lead to his downfall."

In 1960, Dorothy Henson, who taught social science, made a notation that McDowell "… tries very hard and should go some place in life. There were no bad conduct marks on McDowell's school record from the time he entered the Drew School until he graduated in 1960.[81]

About McDowell's family, the investigator learned that "Son McDowell, who is Cleve's father, had always been considered a good old trusted colored man. They say Son and his wife worked on the farm for Mr. R. K. Sage until Mr. Sage died and then continued working for Mr. Hubert Sage, who is the son of R. K. Sage, until the old man began to get too old to work on the farm. Son McDowell is an old Negro, perhaps around 80. Ozett, the mother … is much younger … the McDowell's own their own home in the Negro section of Drew."

It was Scarbrough's "personal opinion" that the NAACP assisted in McDowell's education – "if they did not pay all of his college expenses for the purpose of using him, since his record appears to be clean."

The investigator was sent back to Drew on June 4 and 5 to find more dirt on young McDowell. From R. D. Cartledge, "cashier of the Bank of Drew," Scarbrough learned that "a Negro female school teacher gave Cleve McDowell a check for $10 payable to McDowell on May 27.... McDowell endorsed the check to Medgar W. Evers [who] in turn cashed the check at a service station in Jackson." This fact was duly reported back to the Sovereignty Commission.

Scarbrough was not able to learn why "Jessie Singleton Gresham" gave McDowell the $10 check. He tried to talk once again to McDowell's father and when he "could get no one to respond to my knock of their front door" he "journeyed over to Oxford ... to observe his admittance to the University School of Law on June 5, 1963." The investigator spent the day with Sheriff Joe Ford "driving around the campus" to see what was going on:

> I observed a number of armed troopers on and about the
> campus. I was told there were 350 specially trained riot
> troopers on the campus. I have no doubt that there were at
> least that many. I also observed a large number of U. S.
> Marshals present. [Otherwise] I did not observe anything
> else unusual ... however, there was feeling of anxiety as to
> whether or not McDowell's entrance would be opposed by
> Governor Barnett. After it became known that [the
> governor] would not personally oppose his entry this feeling
> relaxed. Of course, everyone shared Governor Barnett's
> feeling and thinking that the government was illegally
> forcing Cleve McDowell's admittance ... but they felt that it
> would do no good to oppose his entry, due to the fact the
> U. S. Government was prepared to enroll McDowell
> irrespective of the feelings of our Governor, and all of the
> white people of this state which were in opposition to
> McDowell's entry to their all-white university.

Sheriff Joe Ford stated that Governor Barnett's decision not to oppose McDowell's entry to the university was wise as "... everyone in the nation knew full well what [his] feelings were concerning the matter of a Negro going to an all-white university and that to oppose his entry could only spell out trouble for all concerned.... I heard many other comments from citizens as well as other officers at the University. All were favorable in thinking Governor Barnett made the right decision in McDowell's case.... It is my observation that everyone resented McDowell being admitted ... but were reconciled to this fact that so long as the Kennedys are in power that situations of this kind will have to be endured by the white people of this state.[82]

Other black students, nearly "a dozen," were supposed to enroll with McDowell at the University of Mississippi Law School, but "they all pulled out in the end" and McDowell was left to face it alone.

> We were trying to integrate the Mississippi schools, the Alabama schools and the Arkansas schools. School integration was ... necessary to get full equality. That was going to be the great savior for us. Meredith had gone into the undergraduate school, and ... that was why I went to the law school.

> People like Alexanders [phonetic], he was supposed to go in with me. We went to get him that night, and his mother cried and carried on. I think he had his bags packed, literally, and he couldn't go.

> I wound up going by myself. Of course, at the time I was brave. We weren't scared of anything. We would take on the world. We were militants, as such. We didn't believe the white folk would kill you then, but we know better now.

Oh, we were ready…. It was winner take all. We weren't taking any back seats.[83]

At Oxford, McDowell was greeted with expected hostility:

It was the height of racial tension. We just had the Ole Miss riots. See, I was involved with Meredith back and forth that whole period of time. Everything that you heard on TV, it was just that bad, and worse, if you were actually there.

Most students – most of them – knew it was hands-off, but there was still the heckling and the isolation. In fact, when I moved into one of the dormitories, everybody else moved out. You had all of the hostility and threats that normally accompany school integration. And all these people now who say that they were there with me were probably there throwing rocks or something.

But keep in mind, we had the marshals and the U. S. Army there at that time, so it wasn't until I got in trouble later, when I was there by myself. But with the Meredith time frame, both of us were there. We had the Army and the marshals and all of that. But then they just packed up and left after Meredith left, and then that left me there by myself.[84]

"What was it like?" McDowell was asked during an oral history interview by Owen Brooks on August 11, 1995: "Well, it was as bad as you could imagine, but at the time we felt like we had to do it. It was a sacrifice that not only I but other people were making. Lucy in Alabama and Hamilton Holmes … who died. There were people who were doing this all over the country, so it wasn't just something that I was the only person doing. It was something that we felt that we had to do."[85]

While the U. S. marshals were on campus, McDowell and Meredith had protection. But when McDowell was left alone, he had to ensure his survival. "I guess you could say I was one of the original militants. I wasn't about to let anybody catch me on the drive back and forth to Drew situation and run me off the road, because they would follow you and honk at you and all of this stuff anyhow. But if some of them had tried to grab me in a bathroom or walking down an alley or something, they probably would have had—they would have gotten an adequate response."

McDowell carried a gun in the car "going back and forth" to his home as did many other Ole Miss Students:

> The college kids had all kind of deer guns and everything you could imagine in their rooms mounted on walls, and several of them had even shot each other, so that wasn't a big deal. But basically, I was just singled out…. Of course, they probably saved my life by putting me out, because, you know…. Medgar Evers was actually assassinated while I was at the university. Then the summer after, the three civil rights workers down in Philadelphia. Any other numbers of people were killed at various points in between – so they [Ole Miss] probably saved my life.[86]

Other black students followed in McDowell's footsteps, years later obtaining their law degrees from Ole Miss. "When Reuben Anderson and Miller and all those guys got there, it was safe. Integration was accepted, because the undergraduate school was well integrated and the schools across the South and the country were fully integrated, or certainly substantially integrated as compared to what had been," McDowell told interviewers:

Rogers: How did you feel when you were getting this treatment at Ole Miss?

McDowell: Well, you know, the thing was, it didn't bother me, because I believed in what I was doing. It was just something that had to be done. We were taught at that time, you know, "Forgive them for they know not what they do," and we just basically recognized that it was something that had to be done and that we felt that we were right and dedicated.

Rogers: How did it happen that you got thrown out? Did somebody just find the gun in your car or—

McDowell: Okay. Well, somebody, I think, probably—well, they knew I had it, because you know how the network goes, and someone supposedly saw me put it in my pocket or take it out of my pocket or something at the car. But the bottom line was that when I ordered the thing from the catalog – at the time, you could order from catalog – and it came to the railroad station or wherever it was over to Cleveland, my name stood out just like anything, and it was orchestrated all the way up.

Rogers: So the station master or whoever was taking—

McDowell: The PDs and the other people, they knew what was going on.

Rogers: They knew all of the black people who had guns?

McDowell: Well, I wasn't the only one who had guns, because, you know—but what I'm saying is, in the school situation, that was the only thing that made it peculiar. But a lot of black people were defending themselves, or would have defended themselves, if it had become necessary. Everybody wasn't just meek and humble and totally nonviolent. At a point, we defended ourselves. You know, the Vernon Daimers [phonetic] and people like that shot back. It wasn't as though we were just like sheep being led to slaughter.

Rogers: We've talked to a number of folks whose families had weapons.

McDowell: Oh, yeah. My daddy had a double-barrel shotgun that hung on two branches that was always loaded. And, you know, the old night rider thing. If they had come to our house, they would have had a go-for.

Rogers: So when they found this, they just bopped you out? Did they expel you then?

McDowell: Oh, yeah. I think I was arrested. They called the county sheriff over and I was arrested, and then they fined me something, fifteen dollars or twenty-five dollars or whatever the fine was for having a gun. And then we had the bogus administrative hearing. There was a federal lawsuit, you know, which the NAACP just didn't pursue past the district court level, because they could have won it if they had pursued it, but they just backed off.

Brooks: Did they send somebody to the hearing?

McDowell: Yeah, Derrick Bell, who later became a federal judge. See, our other cases had been Motley, Constance Motley had handled—and Thurgood Marshall had been involved with the early phases of some of these cases that got us into Ole Miss.

McDowell's expulsion from the University of Mississippi on September 24 came at the recommendation of the student Judicial Council, "returning [the university] to the Deep South state its unique system of totally segregated public schools."[87] After the decision was announced, McDowell said he had "no emotion to express whatsoever at this time."[88]

"Champ Tierney," the son-in-law of Senator Eastland, headed the Student Judicial Council that tried and expelled McDowell according to Sovereignty Commission reports. McDowell's attorney, R. Jess Brown had to sneak out of town afterwards on back roads after his life was threatened.

Nearly 200 students gathered silently in front of the campus cafeteria to watch McDowell's departure. "Campus police would not allow newsmen to talk to McDowell at the university but he was questioned briefly at a service station where he stopped for gasoline." Speaking "exclusively" with a reporter from the school newspaper, McDowell was asked about his reluctance to issue statements. "That's very simple," he replied. "I'm not a leader in any movement. I'm a student of law and I'm pursuing a law degree." Governor Barnett from his Jackson office refused comment.[89]

One year later, McDowell asked a federal court to reinstate him, contending officials used prejudiced standards in his expulsion. After researching the issue of guns at Ole Miss, McDowell found that thirty-four white Ole Miss students had guns confiscated from them during the past school year and they were not expelled. McDowell listed each student by name and asked that their records be produced by court order.[90]

Guns were also found in a fraternity house during the "Battle of Oxford" where [Mississippi U. S. Senator] Trent Lott, a popular student leader, cheerleader, and president of the Sigma Nu fraternity, was an ardent segregationist. Lott was singled out for praise by Sigma Nu's national board for keeping his frat brothers away from the fighting even though federal authorities seized two dozen firearms (shotguns, rifles and pistols) in a raid on the Sigma Nu house on the day after the campus insurrection. No charges were ever lodged against the fraternity or its members.[91]

Author Bill Doyle in looking over the events at Ole Miss, questioned why the guns were there in the first place. Who put them there? Did Lott know about the guns and why was there a need for university officials to approve a search for and seizure of the guns by the U. S. Army combat troops?

To Doyle, the "most baffling mystery of all" is how Trent Lott could have been at the epicenter of such a violent and tragic event without quickly coming to peace with the idea of treating African-Americans as full American citizens.

"Instead, it seems to have embittered his segregationist views — two years later he supported the cause of keeping blacks out of the national Sigma Nu fraternity."

McDowell said of the Thurgood Marshall School of Law at Texas Southern University, where he went to finish his law degree in 1969 and where he was president of the student bar association,

… It was a Movement school. The great black lawyers were teaching us the things we needed to know [for civil rights litigation]. R. Jess Brown had graduated from Texas Southern, and I worked with him for a while [I was] in Jackson, too. But that was probably why I went to Texas Southern, because R. Jess Brown had gone to Texas Southern in order to practice law in Mississippi. He was one of the original three black lawyers in the state - Jack Young, Sr., R. Jess Brown, and Carsie Hall were the original three black lawyers, and all of the civil rights cases had to have one of them attached as local counsel. So when all the people from Harvard and everywhere else came in here—Derrick Bell, Thurgood Marshall, Connie Motley—all those people had to attach themselves to one of these three lawyers in order to represent people in the state.[92]

McDowell still had to pass the Mississippi bar in order to practice law in his home state. Graduates of The University of Mississippi School of Law had diploma privileges, "and of course, you could not get into the university because it was segregated, and you couldn't pass the bar unless they wanted you to. So they had effectively blocked out-of-staters and blacks." Once Ole Miss integrated the law school, it meant that black lawyers could finally acquire diploma privileges "just like the white students were, and a few years later they changed it and made everybody start taking the state bar."[93] McDowell had initial problems with the Mississippi Bar Association when his admission was first refused. But he won the fight on May 1, 1971, and was later employed by the bar organization for a short period of time.

At the end of his term, McDowell told Ron Harris of the Associated Press he hoped his appointment helped to pave the way for other African Americans, that he had "pushed hard" to get the appointment because he felt blacks needed to become involved at the decision making level.

In a later interview, McDowell spoke of a need for creating a watchdog group to locate and identify persons responsible for civil rights murders, "just as Nazi war criminals were prosecuted."

"There ought to be some organization to track them down…. Right now some of those people are smiling and grinning in our faces and asking us to vote for them." McDowell did not elaborate.

But stacked in the corner of his Drew office was a growing mound of boxes filled with files holding notes and reports. The same was true of McDowell's coffee table at home: between the two sites were every piece of paper McDowell had collected that had to do with a murder, lynching or some other civil rights-based crime.

McDowell and two other lawyers ("perhaps Texans who went to school with Cleve"[94]) were doing their own investigations – from the murder of Emmett Till and Medgar Evers forward, gathering every piece of information they could lay their hands on to solve crimes against black people, local, state and national.

IN THE SPRING of 1997, Cleve McDowell, described by James Meredith, as a "bright and articulate" civil rights lawyer and activist, was shot and killed in his Drew home on March 13.

McDowell, 55, a former state field director of the Mississippi Conference of the NAACP, had represented clients in civil rights cases over three decades. He was a member of the state Penitentiary Board from 1971 until 1976 and served as state director for Head Start from 1972 to 1976. He was a Sunflower County judge from 1978 to 1982 and ran unsuccessfully for the Legislature in 1978 and 1987.

Hearing the news of McDowell's murder, Myrlie Evers-Williams told *Clarion-Ledger* reporter Eric Stringfellow that she first met McDowell when he was a student at Jackson State involved in the NAACP and "she was speechless" when told of his death.

"All I can say is I'm shocked and saddened. My strongest memories are when he applied to Ole Miss and the difficulties and the harassment and how proud I think the entire community was.

"He was one of the few who would mention Medgar as a role model, and he did it during a time when others wouldn't mention Medgar – either they had forgotten or chose to forget. Whenever Cleve would speak, he would always mention something about Medgar," Evers-Williams said.[95]

"The streets are quieter now in Drew," mused one old friend of McDowell's. "Cleve was so bright and he was a true character. Every so often, he would 'fire' his secretary. She'd stomp home, carrying her pink purse. I can see it now. Sometimes Cleve called out after her, saying he was really sorry and asking her to come back. Other times, he would be seen a few minutes later walking to her house – sort of like he was crawling there begging her to come back to work."

On August 21, 1997, nineteen-year-old Juarez Webb of Indianola was indicted by Sunflower County grand jurors on charges of capital murder and robbery of McDowell. And for several months, the charges stuck.

Cleve McDowell's dead body was discovered in his home by his sister, his office manager Nettie Davis, and a Drew police officer.

McDowell's sister was checking on her brother who did not call her the night before on the telephone, as was his custom, and said she was concerned when she saw the front door ajar. Together the three found McDowell upstairs in his dressing room, leaned up against the wall naked, and covered with a comforter. "It didn't make sense," Davis said.

The city's police chief quickly came to the scene, and according to several witnesses, including Davis, "He told us all to leave the house, including the police officer, and he stayed in the house for a long time, tearing up the floors and walls – like he was looking for something. He walked out with a small sack, but I don't know what he had. It was obvious that he messed up the crime scene before the state investigators could get there."

"About 20 minutes after the police chief's departure, Sunflower County Circuit Judge Gray Evans filed an order to seal the premises of McDowell's residence making discussions of 'any findings or evidence from the crime scene' illegal for any officers and personnel working the crime scene."

The same gag order "remains in effect," even though the investigation was closed years ago, insisted the Sunflower County assistant district attorney Hallie Gail Bridges who in the fall of 2003 refused access to any of the police investigation or court records stored in the courthouse basement in Indianola, even though the gag order never covered court officers.[96] "The family would have to approve first," stated a Sunflower County judge upon receiving a request by this author for case records.

Webb's case files kept in the courthouse were accessible however, and indicated the following:

- An autopsy performed in Jackson that night by Steven T. Hayne, M.D., the state's deputy coroner, indicated "negative" signs of any drug abuse.

- Cause of death was given as a "gunshot wound of the left neck, distant and perforating."

- The death was listed as a homicide.

- Three gunshot wounds fired in "close temporal proximity" but not at close range were described by the coroner: a "nonlethal" wound consisting of a "nonlethal distant and perforating gunshot wound of the left back," a "nonlethal distant and perforating gunshot of the left shoulder with re-entry penetrating gunshot wound of the left temple" and a "lethal distant and perforating gunshot wound of the left neck." These descriptions could not be put into sequential order, the report stated.

- The autopsy report did not give information regarding the range from which the gun was fired, but in 2004, a physician practicing forensic medicine was asked to read the report and give his opinion. The examining physician stated that it appeared the shots could have been fired from fifteen feet away. The physician also speculated there could have been more than one shooter, given the angles of the three shots. Information about all of the bullets causing these wounds was not available in the report. Rumors from Drew are that McDowell was killed with his own gun.

"The police chief was saying awful things about Cleve when he came out of the house. I know that Judge Gray was just trying to tone things down before the gossip got out of hand," Davis said. "But I wouldn't think he meant for the gag order never to be lifted."

Six months after McDowell's murder, a fire occurred in downtown Drew, devastating the town's largest department store and the vacant office next door. All of the records McDowell had collected over the years from his personal research on unsolved race-based murders and lynchings were stored in the vacant office and reportedly destroyed or removed. (The fire and missing records came in the same week that the Sovereignty Commission was to release its own secret records. It is suggested that some knew of McDowell's records and may have destroyed them rather than let them see the light of day.)

The fire's flames were so high that some Cleveland residents could see the "lighted sky" eleven miles away from Drew. Others reported hearing an "explosion" in Drew at the beginning of the fire. Drew police chief Burner Smith refused to release the records of the fire. Nor would Bridges.

Webb changes plea

Juarez Webb filed a Petition to Enter a Guilty Plea, reducing his plea from capital murder to manslaughter on January 26, 1998. In his request, Webb said he "shot and killed Cleve McDowell, without malice, in the heat of passion" and "not in necessary self-defense." Webb also asserted that he was earlier "coerced" into pleading guilty to manslaughter by his attorneys:

"They told me I wasn't going to be able – I wasn't going to be able to get nowhere in this case, that I might as well go ahead and take a plea; otherwise, it would be over with me…. I guess they were talking about my life."

But on July 22, 1998, Webb reversed himself and filed a jailhouse petition to withdraw his guilty plea, citing "a series of interrogations, threats and promises [made to him] by various law enforcement officials" and "a series of statements of an incriminating nature [that were] obtained from Petitioner in taped, written and oral form against the Petitioner's will and consent [sic]."[97]

Interrogations, Webb claimed, were "unsolicited" and "initiated by … the instance [sic] of arresting officers and other varies [sic] courthouse officials." Webb said he did not waive his rights to silence or counsel or self-incrimination, but that he was forced unwillingly and without counsel present to answer questions.

Webb said he was "repeatedly interrogated and threatened as well as coerced to admit to the crime in an involuntary nature, thus rendering his guilty plea involuntary as the result of being threatened by the officials to receive the death penalty." Courthouse records indicate that Webb was taken for a psychological examination to determine if he was potentially suicidal.

Appointed counsel, Webb went to trial on January 27, 1998 and "maintained his innocence," his petition states. His family was "repeatedly harassed by law enforcement officials and was told by his attorneys that he would get the death penalty if he did not take a plea for a lesser charge of manslaughter."

Webb asserted the charge of capital murder was dropped to manslaughter "due to the pressure and threats and unlawful statements obtained as well as other evidence and unlawful arrest against his will."

Webb also admitted giving "false statements in court to end the truma [sic] and nightmare and to protect his family from further threats and harassments … [the] guilty pleas was made unwillingly, involuntarily and [he] was coerced to give his plea to avoid a big trial and publicity on his family." What Webb wanted was permission to withdraw his plea of guilty and to prove his innocence "so that the real suspect can be caught."

At the time of his slaying, McDowell was Webb's court-appointed attorney on earlier burglary charges. "The police thought Webb killed Cleve to steal his Cadillac, money and jewelry. It was all missing from his home when his body was found. They said Webb confessed to the killing when he was arrested," a friend said.

At Webb's preliminary hearing, according to a *Clarion-Ledger* account, Drew Police Chief Burner Smith testified that Webb, 18, told police "McDowell had thrown him on the floor and tried to pull his pants down to sexually assault him." Also, "District Attorney Carlton said accepting Webb's plea was the best decision" since the case was "not iron-clad" and that McDowell "needed to be remembered for what he did as a leader in the Civil Rights Movement at a time when that wasn't too popular."

Webb did not get what he had hoped for. On July 9, 1999, Circuit Judge Gray Evans denied and dismissed his motion. Gray wrote that it had "probably" been a "wise" recommendation by Webb's attorney to urge Webb to plead guilty to manslaughter rather than face the possibility of a death sentence from a conviction of capital murder.

So many questions remain unanswered. There are a moderate number of records in the Sovereignty Commission files on McDowell; most reports are harmless. His former office manager said that McDowell received some of the reports to look over before they were made public, but did not appear disturbed over the information obtained. One last record gave the name of a possible Jackson "homosexual partner," and also declared McDowell as a young black man on the rise – someone who impressed the Governor.

As Davis spoke about McDowell's murder, she remembered something that struck her as unusual: "When Cleve was murdered, the strangest thing to me was how neat the coffee table looked. I went into the house with Cleve's sister and that was the first thing I noticed.

"It was always a mess, with papers, files, and books stacked up and even falling off. Everyone who knew him would remember that table. But that morning it looked like it had been cleaned up when we went into the house. Every paper was stacked neatly in a pile.

"There were these neat piles all over the table. My eye caught the coffee table immediately, as soon as I walked in. I had never seen it like this before," Davis said.

Retired funeral home employee Woodrow Jackson of Tutwiler backed up Davis's assertion. That McDowell's coffee table was straightened the day his body was discovered, Jackson found intriguing.

"This says something. His coffee table was always very messy. He would never have straightened it up, himself. I didn't see his body, but from what I could reconstruct from the rumors going around, there might have been two people involved in the shooting."

Jackson, who embalmed Emmett Till in 1955, talked softly. "I knew Cleve very well. I didn't embalm his body; I believe it was someone from Cleveland who did. But Cleve was a good lawyer and we often spoke about Emmett Till because he was so interested in finding all who were involved in the murder.

"Cleve kept boxes of records in his office. I know, because I saw them. I remember a year or so ago before Cleve was murdered he brought Emmett Till up again and still seemed upset, but he would never give out any details. When his office burned down after he was murdered, a lot of important papers had to have been lost."[98]

Still another person who knew McDowell responded with surprise over his cleaned-up coffee table. "Now that means something," Margaret Block said. Block, from Cleveland, said she was getting ready to have McDowell do some legal work for her. "I was very surprised when he was killed, but I had never heard any of these details until now, including that his coffee table was cleaned up."[99]

Nettie Davis also noticed that all of McDowell's guns appeared to be missing. "He had guns in many places throughout the house and his office. He was always within reach of a gun. I don't know how he could have been so surprised, as to have been shot. I never learned what happened to all of his guns in his house or in his office. He also kept guns in his car."

The FBI, responding to a Freedom of Information request, first asserted it has no records on McDowell – strange, since several close friends say that FBI agents "more than once" visited McDowell's office in the years before his death. Later, several records were sent by the FBI regarding a minor incident during McDowell's tenure as a Tunica Judge.

One Drew friend said he always believed McDowell's murder might be related to a "very large" settlement he won for a client who lived near Tunica and "may have involved something to do with a utility company." Several other friends confirmed this story.

McDowell had invited this friend and his wife to dinner shortly before he was murdered. "He said he had won 'the big' case he'd been working on and for once had lots of money. I didn't know anything about this case, but I did hear that no attorney in Memphis would take it. Some say there might have been mob involvement."

There is still another story deserving attention that may relate to McDowell's murder. Two close friends independently recalled an incident that took place about four years before McDowell's death: McDowell had learned that a close friend, Henry S. Mims, an Alabama lawyer who grew up in Drew had "committed suicide." McDowell's immediate reaction was that it would be impossible for Mims to have killed himself; it wasn't in his personality.[100]

Several Drew friends were set to drive to Alabama for the funeral, but McDowell suggested he would "go out first and try to find out what happened."

Paying a visit to Mims' widow before the funeral, McDowell asked for permission to view the body, but she refused. She also said the casket would be closed for the funeral, McDowell later told his minister.

McDowell would not have taken such news sitting down, but most likely went to the funeral home and found the body, his friend said. "He would find out what happened to Mims. He would never take 'no' for an answer."

From Montgomery, Alabama, McDowell phoned a friend back in Drew to report seeing Mims' body with "cuts and broken fingers." Something was very wrong with the suicide story, he told a friend.

McDowell planned driving back to Drew and said he would not stay for the funeral. He also suggested that his friends not drive to Alabama, as planned, but stay home. "He told me this was not going to be open casket and that he was angry with his friend's wife. He also said something was very wrong."

McDowell's friends went to the funeral, anyway and were surprised at "all of the California people" who attended. "So many, that most of his other friends could not get inside of the church." Mims was a graduate of the City College of Los Angeles, and apparently had maintained contact with the Californians.

When McDowell arrived back in Drew, he told his minister there was no evidence of a suicide and that Mims showed signs of torture; he'd been found by his wife, "hanging from a ladder inside of his garage," but "the whole thing looked like a setup to make his murder look like a suicide."[101]

Then McDowell said something strange, something "out of character," according to his minister. "He asked me to promise I would conduct his funeral when the time should come – and he meant it," the minister said.

"I thought he was kidding at first, and I told him I would be dying before he would since I'm quite a bit older. But he was serious and he looked scared. I asked him if he knew what happened to Mims and if he knew who did it. He said yes, and then looked down and said nothing else."

For the next four years, McDowell – also a Baptist minister – decreased his time spent working in his law office, instead working at building his own church congregation.

"He would spend more time picking out the dishes and other special purchases for the church than coming to work," recounted Nettie Davis, who also confirmed some parts of the "Alabama funeral" story.

"Sometime I'd get worried and tell Cleve 'we' might get sued,'" she laughed. "He just really changed after the Alabama trip, and it was so important for him that everything be done exactly right for the new church. That mattered to him more than anything else."

Mims had been to Drew visiting friends and family only a few weeks before he died. "He looked fine. He was happy and I remember we all had dinner together," Davis' husband said. All but one of Mims and McDowell's relatives living in Drew refused to be interviewed.

NEARLY ALL OF McDowell's friends requested anonymity when asked to talk about his murder. One friend, a former Parchman prison guard, explained: "Most of us know that Cleve's death was not just a matter of a young kid shooting him because he thought Cleve was trying to molest him.

"That would be impossible, anyway, because Webb was too old, legally, to be molested.... But, there had been FBI hanging around here, and I personally think Cleve had to be one of the reasons why.... His family and friends, I think, are still afraid to talk. They know what it is still like in the Delta, and so do I [since] I know how some of the richest people work."[102]

The former Parchman guard, speaking only on the condition of anonymity, stated that in 1962, when James Meredith was attempting to enter the University of Mississippi, he [the prison guard] was approached by a "rich, white planter" who "tried to hire" him "to kill Meredith."

"He wanted me to 'do something' about Meredith. Of course, I said no. But that is how it has always been around here – rich white people paying off others, including blacks, to murder black people. They think this keeps us in line."[103]

Mississippi attorney Constance Slaughter who was quoted in *The Clarion-Ledger* at the time of McDowell's death, refused an interview when contacted, becoming angry enough to hang up the telephone.[104]

Charles McLauren of Indianola, an active civil rights advocate and SNCC member who knew McDowell did not want to talk either, and deferred to McDowell's family. Conceding that family members would not talk about McDowell, McLaurin offered, "They think it's better to let a sleeping dog lie."

It is the "gay" issue that keeps many friends and family from talking about McDowell, McLaurin confirmed before ending the call.[105]

One young man interviewed in Drew, also requesting anonymity, claimed that he had been "molested" by McDowell "for years" and "wish I'd shot him, myself."[106]

But he also said that an attempt to "make [McDowell] look like a pedophile" had been a set-up. Cleveland parents of a young child made the accusation, but no charges were ever filed. The interviewee, who said he also knew Webb, asserted that Webb told him he'd "had sex with McDowell first and then shot him afterwards He did not say he was molested." This interviewee also stated that FBI personnel were in Drew "by noon" after McDowell's body was discovered. "They had been watching him," he said, but gave no details.[107]

* * *

WHAT OF THE "gay issue"? Rumors persist that McDowell and several other "well-known" Civil Rights veterans were gay.

Sovereignty Commission files show that agents often jumped at any chance to report (by name) the alleged gay behavior of blacks. Yet rumors still circulate that Governor Ross Barnett, white, and a Citizens Council member, was gay and "slept with at least one well-known black activist."

Professor John Howard of Queen's College in London offered an insight to gay activities in the Mississippi Delta during the Civil Rights Movement in his thesis on "[T]he love that dare not speak its name in the Bible belt." Howard's academic paper was turned into a popular press book, *Men Like That*, as the author worked to "debunk the myth that same-sex desires can't find expression outside the big city."

Nominally conservative institutions of small town life – home, church, school, and workplace – were the "very sites where queer sexuality flourished," Howard responded through an e-mail interview.[108] "Far more" is to be discovered: "It's still early days for Southern lesbian, gay, bisexual, and transgender (LGBT) history. We've only begun to scratch the surface."

QUESTION: To what extent did race place a role in selection of sexual partners in homosexual men and women in Mississippi in civil rights and pre-civil rights days?

HOWARD: I'm thinking of Gov. Ross Barnett ... since the rumours are still thick. Generally speaking, before the 1960s, LGBT Southerners, black and white, participated in similar practices and networks. But they were doing so in two parallel, segregated worlds. If gender and sexual non-conformity had to be very carefully negotiated, then all the more so if it involved interracial interaction. That's not to say that there was no interracial homosexual activity before the civil rights era. Obviously, it was easier for whites to approach blacks. And of course we have more evidence of that.

Some have even suggested that many elite white males in particular assumed access to black male bodies, in the way that, since slavery, they had expected access to black females.

Especially illuminating here is William Armstrong Percy III's article about his kinsman, William Alexander Percy, with whom I'm sure you're familiar. The article appears in my edited collection, "Carryin' On in the Lesbian and Gay South" (New York University Press, 1997). That, along with what I've written in "Men Like That, "is about as much as we know at this point about queer history in the Delta.

Aaron Henry is probably an exception, not the rule, when it comes to black-white gay activity. There were few with his level of power, few who would have taken the risk of approaching a white male. His life history also demonstrates that at least some young white gay Southerners would have been willing to engage in interracial, intergenerational, homosexual activity.

That is, they would have been able to ignore all the social norms and taboos – those which described blacks as inferior, older people as undesirable. And of course we have evidence to suggest that those willing to combat racial injustice and get involved in the Civil Rights Movement may have been more willing to challenge prevailing sexual attitudes and values as well.

QUESTION: Nobody who really knew Cleve McDowell wants to talk, even now. While he was probably gay, the evidence I've collected shows he was shot in the back and possibly by two shooters. Why won't his friends and family get past this to try and find out who murdered him?

HOWARD: A deep-rooted and longstanding homosexual homicide mythology associates gay men with dangerous lifestyles and disgraceful deaths. Further, up until the late 1960s, homosexuality in the South was largely accommodated with pretence of ignorance, a system of mutual discretion in which much was understood but left unsaid. To this day, many rely on that quiet accommodationism, preferring silence or subtlety over open confrontation, despite all the hooping and hollering of evangelical ministers.

That's a very recent phenomenon. Protestant ministers in the South didn't begin railing against homosexuality, at least in large numbers, until the late 1960s and early 1970s. I'd be curious to know more about your evidence on McDowell, especially the notion that he was "perhaps a pedophile." Of course, his enemies would have wanted that sort of idea to circulate. But do you have proof that he had sexual intercourse with children? With pre-pubescent youth? It's worth mentioning that the legal age of consent here in Great Britain is sixteen for both heterosexual and homosexual sex. Are you sure McDowell's partners were incapable of consenting? I mention this because such accusations are a classic form of intimidation by white supremacists.

Bill Higgs, as you know, was accused of having sex with a sixteen-year-old. This may have been true. But it also may have involved what I would refer to as a set of consensual acts. You need only look back several decades to find a time when the age of consent in Southern states was what would now be seen as shockingly low. [The statutory age of sexual consent was increased from 14 to 16 in Mississippi as of January 1, 2000.]

VI. Lists of the Dead: Civil rights, racial slayings and missing persons suspected as dead in Mississippi

The names of some people killed in Mississippi and listed on the Southern Poverty Law Center's Civil Rights Memorial. (Many names are missing.)

The Rev. George Lee, Belzoni, May 7, 1955.

Lamar Smith, Brookhaven, August 13, 1955.

Emmett Louis Till, Money, August 28, 1955.

Mack Charles Parker, Poplarville, April 25, 1959.

Herbert Lee, Liberty, September 25, 1961.

Cpl. Roman Ducksworth Jr., April 9, Taylorsville.

Paul Guihard, Oxford, September 30, 1962.

Medgar Evers, Jackson, June 12, 1963.

Louis Allen, Liberty, April 7, 1964.

Henry Hezekiah Dee and Charles Eddie Moore, Meadville, May 2, 1964.

James Earl Chaney, Andrew Goodman and Michael Schwerner, Philadelphia, June 21, 1964.

Vernon Dahmer, Hattiesburg, January 10, 1966.

Ben Chester White, Natchez, June 10, 1966.

Warlest Jackson, Natchez, February 27, 1967.

Benjamin Brown, Jackson, May 12, 1967.

The names of people killed in Mississippi suspected by the Southern Poverty Law Center as victims of racially motivated murders from 1954 to 1968. Again, the list is incomplete.

Eli Brumfield, McComb, October 31, 1961.

Woodrow Wilson Daniels, Water Valley, July 1, 1958.

William Roy Prather, Corinth, November 1, 1959.

Jonas Causey, Clarksdale, May 10, 1959.

George Love, Ruleville, January 8, 1958.

Charles Brown, Yazoo City, June 25, 1957.

Milton Russell, Belzoni, January 21, 1956.

Edward Duckworth, Raleigh, January 1956.

James E. Evanston, near Drew, December 24, 1955.

Izell (or Izeal) Henry, beaten on July 28, 1954, Glendora. Died in 1958 or 1959.

Clinton Melton, Glendora, December 3, 1955.

Willie Joel Lovett, Tchula, June 30, 1963.

Unidentified black woman and two unidentified black men, Woodville, February 1964.

Johnny Queen, Fayette, August 8, 1965.

Ollie W. Shelby, Jackson, January 22, 1965.

Romie Harris, Tupelo, December 30, 1963.

Unidentified black man, in Big Black River in Goodman, September 11, 1963.

Freddie Lee Thomas Jr., Greenwood, September 3, 1965 or August 20, 1965.

Julius Y. Jones, Laurel, September 4, 1965.

Jimmy Lee Griffin, Sturgis, September 27, 1965.

Robert Joseph McNair, Pelahatchie, November 6, 1965.

Lillie Dell Power, Starkville, November 27, 1965.

Eli Brumfield, McComb, October 13, 1961.

Sylvester Maxwell, Canton, January 17, 1963.

Herbert Oarsby or Hubert Orsby in the Big Black River near Pickens, September 9, 1964.

Unidentified black woman near the Columbus Air Force Base, August 29, 1963.

Unidentified black man shot to death in car, Natchez, March 1964.

Ernest Jells, 21, Clarksdale, September 23, 1963.

Ollie B. Shelby, 18, Hinds County, January 1965.

John Lee, 31, Goshen Springs, February 1965.

Donald Rasbery, 19, Okolona, February 1965.

Willie Henry Lee, 21, Goshen Springs, February 25, 1965.

Jessie Brown, Winona, January 13, 1965.

Saleam K. Triggs, Forest, January 25, 1965.

Curtie Watts, Forest, January 25, 1965.

Robert McNair, Pelahatchie, November 6, 1965.

Separate list of lynched black people in the Delta collected by Joyce Russer of Bolivar County.

James Edward Calhoun, Cleveland, MS, September 8, 1976,
Sunflower County

William Ody, Clayton, July 15, 1902

George Kincaid, Cleveland, June 12, 1903

Fayette Sawyer, Cleveland, March 19, 1904

Burke Harris, Cleveland, March 19, 1904

John Hollins, Drew, January 10, 1903

Willie Webb, Drew, February 23, 1913

Green Jackson, Greenville, February 6, 1891

Burke Martin, Greenville, March 2, 1890

Robert Dennis, Greenville, June 4, 1903

William Robinson, Greenville, August 17, 1909

Peter Henderson, Itta Bena, January 20, 1897

Doc Davis, Jackson, July 19, 1892

Theodore Pickett, Jackson, July 6, 1895

John Gray, Jackson, September 18, 1923

N/A Wimberly, Jackson, June 20, 1921

D. Moore, Jackson, February 7, 1957

Two unidentified blacks, Clarksdale, October 11, 1915

Lindsay Coleman, Clarksdale, December 19, 1925

Charles E. Moore, Jackson, May 2, 1964

Henry Dee, Jackson, May 2, 1964

Henry Askey, Mississippi City, June 9, 1900

Ed Russ, Mississippi City, June 9, 1900

Claude Singleton, Poplarville, April 20, 1918

Robert Keglar's list of missing and presumably dead people ("Mysterious Deaths") from the Delta. Robert of Tallahatchie County lost his mother and brother in 1966 under suspicious circumstances and his story is told in "Where Rebels Roost, Mississippi Civil Rights Revisited," published June 15, 2005.

Maddins, Willie B.

Albert Boss and Annie Ruth Winford

Jack Reynolds

Bonnie Towns

Lesley Jones

John W. Noel

Birdia Keglar

James KIeglar

Gladys Frost

Anedia Trimm

L. D. Gray, Jr.

Ashley Haskins

Adeline Hamlet

Acknowledgements

I owe a debt of gratitude to many people who have helped me write this book and Where Rebels Roost, Mississippi Civil Rights Revisited. I would especially like to thank Nettie Davis and her family for sharing memories of a good friend, Cleve McDowell; Margaret Block for sharing her personal experiences and information about her brother, Sam Block; Dr. L. C. Dorsey for her support and enthusiasm and for sharing her family stories; Benjamin T. Greenberg for his many thoughtful contributions, especially for the time he gave this project in writing a comprehensive and sensitive foreword to this book; Lawrence Guyot for his interest in this project and sharing of resources; Hunter Bear [Dr. John R. Salter, Jr./Hunter Gray] for sharing his memories of Medgar Evers; Marvin Flemmons who shared the blues history he has so carefully gathered; Calvin Stewart for telling me about Birdia Keglar; Robert Keglar, Gwen Dailey and Lucy Boyd for sharing their memories of Birdia Keglar and her son, James; Rev. Willie Blue for information shared on Mrs. Keglar; Charles Sudduth for sharing his early-day experiences in Washington County and his intimate knowledge of the Klan; Jan Hilligas and Geoffrey F.X. O'Connell for special editing help; Mrs. Fairman of Tougaloo College for helping to locate archived materials; Dr. Bill Tucker for writing his book on Scientific Racism that opened up information about the Sovereignty Commission and Mississippi history; "Arrow" for his continued interest and answering so many questions; Kerrie Schoppe for her web work and interest; Betty Orr, John Orr, Bette Smith and Ursula Powers for their ongoing interest; Owen Brooks for listening and introducing Jan Hillegas; Ira Wilson for his ongoing enthusiasm; a minister who remains unnamed who shared an important book that sparked the idea for writing this book; two physicians and a healthcare administrator for their sustained interest and encouragement; another physician, Larry Williamson, who has maintained interest, and so many others whose names do not appear, either by their choice, my concern for their safety or my forgetfulness. Thanks to everyone. Sk

About the Author

Susan Klopfer is the author of "Abort! Retry! Fail!" (Prentice Hall), selected as a Book of-the-Month Club alternate selection. She holds an MBA degree from Indiana Wesleyan University and a BA degree from Hanover College. She is a former acquisitions and development editor for Simon and Schuster (Prentice Hall), and is an award-winning journalist for her investigative reporting in Missouri. She is the pet owner of *Maury* (the gray and white-striped cat).

Book Order Information: Visit http://themiddleoftheinternet.com

End Notes

[1] David M. Oshinsky, "Worse Than Slavery: Parchman Farm and the Ordeal of Jim Crow Justice," (New York: Simon and Schuster, 1996), 230.

[2] Christopher Mettress, ed., "The Lynching of Emmett Till: a Documentary Narrative," (Charlottesville and London: University of Virginia Press, 2002), xiii.

[2] Nikki Davis Maute, "Civil Rights Stories Find Home," *Hattiesburg* American, Feb. 24, 2005.

[3] Avis Thomas-Lester, "Senate Prepares for an Apology Long Overdue: Past efforts to enact anti-lynching law defeated by filibuster," Washington Post, June 13, 2005.

[4] Aaron Henry with Constance Curry, "The Fire Ever Burning," (University Press of Mississippi: Jackson, 2000), 91, 92.

[5] Ibid., 93.

[6] "The Murder of Emmett Till," Part I, Till's Death. Online at About African American History

[http://afroamhistory.about.com/library/weekly/aa021703a.htm].

[7] Ibid.

[8] Ann Waldron, "Hodding Carter, The Reconstruction of a Racist," (Chapel Hill: Algonquin Books of Chapel Hill, 1993), 256.

[9] From an interview with Mr. Jackson by the author in 2004.

[10] "The Murder of Emmett Till," ibid.

[11] From an interview with Nettie Davis of Drew by the author, 2003.

[12] Anne Moody, "Coming of Age in Mississippi," (New York, NY, 1968), 123-126.

[13] Ibid.

[14] Henry, Curry, 95.

[15] Ibid., 95.

[16] Henry, Curry, 96.

[17] Ibid., 96.

[18] Sumner did not stay uneventful. Years later on May 23, 1971, veteran Eddie McClinton was allegedly killed by a white "night marshal" in Sumner in a fight at a pop machine. A Sovereignty Commission investigator learned from county deputy sheriff Downs, doubling as the town marshal, that Aaron Henry sent a telegram to President Richard Nixon over the incident, asserting that McClinton was shot three times and killed by a white outside of Sumner. McClinton was observed by Sumner Night Marshal Tom Trannam "kicking and beating on a change machine" at a self-service gas station. When Trannam intervened, McClinton threatened to kill him, Downs told the investigator. "McClinton started for Trannam, in a threatening manner, Trannam fired one shot to the right of McClinton attempting to stop him.

McClinton continued to advance and told Trannam, 'If you don't kill me, you white S.O.B., I'm going to kill you.' At this time, Trannam shot McClinton once in the arm and once in the chest with a 45 cal. pistol," the investigator's report stated. No hearing or coroner's inquest was held, and Downs said he would get back to the investigator after he conferred with Trannam "and the two negro witnesses."

[19] Conversation with Ada Guest and the author, fall of 2004. We "ran into" Mrs. Guest on a Sunday afternoon in Sumner as she was patrolling the downtown, looking for strangers who needed "help." After she followed our car for a mile or so, I pulled in next to the Cassidy Bayou to see why I was being followed. "You lost?" she asked from her car window. Learning that we were enjoying a Sunday drive to Sumner, she relaxed and soon told us about the trial. For a number of years, Mrs. Guest served on the county's draft board, she said.

[20] Hank Klibanoff, "L. Alex Wilson: A Reporter Who Refused to Run," *Media Studies Journal*, Vol.14 no.2, Spring/Summer 2000.

[21] Ibid.

[22] Results of the autopsy were not released at the time of this book's publication. See updates on the emmett-till.com blogsite.

[23] Waldron, 258.

[24] Ibid.

[25] Ibid., 259.

[26] Mississippi Sovereignty Commission, SCR ID # 99-9-0-72-1-1-1.

[27] Ibid., SCR ID # 2-36-1-8-1-1-1 and SCR ID # 2-30-0-19-1-1-1.

[28] Waldron, 260.

[29] Lomax returned to Mississippi in 1967 for Ramparts magazine to investigate the slaying of Michael Schwerner, James Chaney and Andrew Goodman.

[30] Some close friends of Cleve McDowell believe he was killed under highly suspicious circumstances. This murder is covered extensively in "Where Rebels Roost, Mississippi Civil Rights Revisited," (LuLu, 2005), by Susan Klopfer with Fred Klopfer and Barry Klopfer.

[31] Staff and wire reports, "Till case to be reopened," *Delta Advertiser*, May 12, 2004, 1.

[32] Kevin Johnson and Laura Parker, "Feds Reopen 1955 Racial Slaying Case," *USA Today*, May 10, 2004, *Nation* section.

[33] Ibid.

[34] "Disappearance" of court records is nothing new in Mississippi. On September 8, 1976, sixteen-year-old James Edward Calhoune was lynched and his body found floating in the Sunflower River. His hands were tied behind his back and his neck and nose were broken, according to Margaret Block, a Delta civil rights activist. Calhoune had been shot in the chest. There was a trial and a man reportedly found guilty and later released from prison afterwards. But checking with the courthouse

circuit clerk, there were "no records" at the Sunflower County courthouse, where the trial took place.

[35] Since this announcement, the author has noticed additional Till files added to the Sovereignty Commission's website.

[36] Ibid.

[37] Associated Press, "Feds unearth Emmett Till's casket," *CNN.com*, June 1, 2005, posted 12:35 pm EDT.

[38] Conversation with X and the author, spring of 2005.

[39] Conversation with a Delta business woman, "X", who requested to remain anonymous. April 2005.

[40] Myrlie Evers, with William Peters, "For Us, The Living," (Jackson: University Press of Mississippi, 1967), 174.

[41] From an interview with Delores Melton Gresham by Susan Klopfer, 2004.

[42] Myrlie Evers, 182-183. Evers cites editorial from the *Delta Democrat-Times*.

[43] Interview with Delores Melton Gresham.

[44] Myrlie Evers.

[45] Myrlie Evers, 181-182.

[46] Copy of Associated Press clipped article found at the Clarksdale Library. No date on the copy.

[47] Ibid.

[48] David Halberstam, "The Fifties," (New York: Villard Books, 1993), 440.

[49] Ibid.

[50] Copy of Associated Press article.

[51] Halberstam.

[52] Ibid.

[53] Copy of unidentified newspaper clipping from the Clarksdale Public Library.

[54] John Dittmer, "Local People," (Urbana and Chicago: University of Illinois Press, 1995), 59, citing David Halberstam.

[55] Bill Minor, "American Experience, Online Forum," *PBS online*, January 23, 2003.

[56] PBS documentary aired February 6, 2005, "February One: The Story of the Greensboro Four," filmmakers Dr. Steven Channing and Rebecca Cerese.

[57] On Monday, May 17, 1954 – the day which many white Southerners remember as "Black Monday" – the United States Supreme Court unanimously outlawed legally imposed racial segregation in public schools in *Brown v. Board of Education of Topeka, Kansas*. "Resenting this voice of American conscience raised by the nation's highest tribunal, some white Southerners advocated that segregation, crucial to their cherished "southern way of life" was God-ordained and some, even though they were small in number, resorted to violence to defend the region's racial status quo. Still, others resurrected a more sophisticated theory of states' rights constitutionalism to defy the Supreme Court decree and to combat the ever-

156

intensifying civil rights movement in the South." [Yasuhiro Katagiri, *The Mississippi State Sovereignty Commission: Civil Rights and States' Rights* (2001)].

[58] "Sovereignty Commission Online Agency History," Mississippi Department of Archives and History, online [http://www.mdah.state.ms.us/arlib/contents/er/index.html].

[59] Erle Johnston, "Mississippi's Defiant Years, 1953-1973: An Interpretive Documentary with Personal Experiences," (1990).

[60] "Sovereignty Commission Online Agency History," ibid.

[61] February 8, 1965, memo concerning files purge and investigation procedure SCR ID # 99-62-0-33-1-1-1.

[62] Cloyte Murdock Larsson, "Land of the Emmett Till Murder Revisited," *Ebony*, March 1986.

[63] From copies of news articles found at the Indianola Library. No dates were apparent.

[64] Woodruff, 138-139. Author cites the *Drew Leader*, Dec. 21, 1923.

[65] Oral history of L. C. Dorsey.

[66] Nan Woodruff, "American Congo," (Cambridge: Harvard University Press, 2003), 138.

[67] Woodruff, 138-139. Woodruff cites the *Drew (Miss) Leader*, December 21, 1923.; see also Chana Kai Lee, "For Freedom's Sake: The Life of Fannie Lou Hamer," (Urbana: University of Illinois Press,1999), 16-18.

[68] Nan Woodruff, author of *American Congo*, writes that "…inspired by the Russian Revolution of 1917, some war-weary workers and soldiers organized strikes in 1917 and 1919 that challenged the monarchies and democracies alike. England and France experienced anti-colonial uprisings…The United States did not escape the upheaval the war had wrought. In 1919 violence and terror erupted across the nation as the federal government moved to destroy the momentum of labor…In Phillips County, Arkansas, this struggle directly challenged planter dominance, triggering a massacre in October of 1919 of hundreds of African American men, women, and children." (74)

[69] Woods, 138-139. Cites Lomas, 1993, 206-7, 468, the *Drew (Miss) Leader*, December 21, 1923.; see also Chana Kai Lee, "For Freedom's Sake: The Life of Fannie Lou Hamer," (Urbana: University of Illinois Press,1999), 16-18.

[70] Woods, 93.

[71] Ibid., 94. Cites Donald Spivey, "Schooling for the New Slavery: Black Industrial Education, 1868-1915," (Westport, CT: Greenwood Press), 74.

[72] Cohodas, 104. Cites United Press International, "Barnett Decides Against Turning Away Second Negro at Mississippi University," The *Edwardville Intelligencer*, June 5, 1963.

[73] Cohodas, 104-105.

[74] I was told by a University employee that the Law School at Ole Miss has a letter in its Cleve McDowell file containing a warm, positive letter of recommendation by the late Dean Farley to the Texas law school, regarding McDowell. When I asked the current Dean's secretary to see the letter in the fall of 2004, for possible use in this book, she said it did not exist. No attempt was made to search for the letter. I fear it has been trashed and is one more example of record-keeping practices in Mississippi.

[75] Oral history interview with Cleve McDowell by Owen Brooks, August 11, 1995. Tougaloo Archives.

[76] Ibid.

[77] Ibid.

[78] Ibid. Stories of "Dewey Ross" still abound and were even spread over into Northern Arkansas. Most people called him "Ross," instead of Roth, his real name, according to Delta blues and Drew historian, Marvin Flemmons.

[79] Oral history interview with Cleve McDowell.

[80] Sovereignty Commission report dated May 31, 1963. Prepared by Tom Scarbrough, investigator. SCR ID # 1-75-0-5-1-1-1.

[81] Ibid.

[82] Sovereignty Commission report dated June 18, 1963. Prepared by Tom Scarbrough, investigator.

[83] Oral history with Cleve McDowell.

[84] Ibid.

[85] Ibid.

[86] Ibid.

[87] UPI, "Mississippi Status Again 'All White,'" The *Holland Evening Sentinal*, September 25, 1963.

[88] Ibid.

[89] Cliff Session, "Had Reason For Gun," *UPI*, undated copy.

[90] UPI, "McDowell Seeks UM Admittance," *Clarion-Ledger*, June 26, 1964.

[91] Joe Conason's Journal, "The Night Trent Lott Did The 'Right thing'," *Salon*, December 19, 2002.

[92] Oral history interview with Cleve McDowell.

[93] Obid.

[94] From a telephone interview with the Godson of Cleve McDowell, Kwasi McDowell, by Susan Klopfer in the fall of 2004. McDowell said that his uncle never talked about what he was working on, except for one time. Kwasi McDowell said he was writing a civil rights paper for school and Cleve McDowell was helping him. While he was writing, Cleve McDowell looked away and quietly said, "People in this state would be surprised if they knew about all the politicians and their families who have murdered people." ... "He didn't say anything else, but he looked upset."

Kwasi McDowell also stated that Cleve may have been working with two lawyers in Texas at one time to track down civil rights murderers. "I think both of those lawyers died in car wrecks, but I don't recall any specifics. I'm not sure if this is true or not."

[95] Eric Stringfellow, "McDowell may have been killed by teen client," *The Clarion-Ledger*, March 15, 1997, 3-B.

[96] It was no secret that McDowell and the assistant district attorney had a difficult relationship. "Cleve would do things like wiggle his tongue in her face when he beat her in court, which was often. I'd tell him to be nicer, but he really liked to upset her," laughed McDowell's former office manager during an interview in 2004. Possibly compounding the difficult relationship, the ADA was an Ole Miss graduate.

[97] The Petition (No. 97-0109) to the Circuit Court of Sunflower County is date-stamped July 22, 1998 and signed by the circuit clerk.

[98] Interview with Woodrow Wilson Jackson.

[99] Conversation with Margaret Block, April 2005

[100] The story of Henry S. Mimms was told to the author in 2004 by two independent sources, both friends of McDowells'.

[101] A circuit court employee in Huntsville Alabama who said she knew Mims, as well, stated in April 2005 during a telephone interview with the author that while Mims "officially committed suicide," many of his friends in Alabama had questioned this medical explanation for the cause of death. "There were a lot of rumors going around at the time," she said. The woman said she was not comfortable repeating any rumors, however.

[102] Interview by Susan Klopfer with former Parchman guard, November 2004. This person asked to remain anonymous.

[103] Ibid.

[104] Telephone conversation with Constance Slaughter, 2003.

[105] Telephone conversation with Charles McLauren, November 3, 2004.

[106] During the time I've been working on this book, I have run into five other people who told me or strongly inferred that Cleve was a "homosexual," including two Sunflower County attorneys, a Drew resident who did not know him personally, an officer of the Circuit Court, and a prison guard who said she knew him and Webb, as well.

[107] Conversation in January of 2005 with a black male in Drew who asked he remain anonymous.

[108] John Howard, "Men Like That: A Southern Queer History," (London: The University of Chicago Press, 1999).